UNLCK

Second Edition

3

Listening, Speaking & Critical Thinking

STUDENT'S BOOK

Sabina Ostrowska and Nancy Jordan
with Chris Sowton, Jennifer Farmer
and Janet Gokay

CAMBRIDGE
UNIVERSITY PRESS

CAMBRIDGE
UNIVERSITY PRESS

University Printing House, Cambridge CB2 8BS, United Kingdom

One Liberty Plaza, 20th Floor, New York, NY 10006, USA

477 Williamstown Road, Port Melbourne, VIC 3207, Australia

314–321, 3rd Floor, Plot 3, Splendor Forum, Jasola District Centre, New Delhi – 110025, India

79 Anson Road, #06–04/06, Singapore 079906

Cambridge University Press is part of the University of Cambridge.

It furthers the University's mission by disseminating knowledge in the pursuit of education, learning and research at the highest international levels of excellence.

www.cambridge.org
Information on this title: www.cambridge.org/9781108659109

© Cambridge University Press 2019

First published 2014
Second Edition 2019

20 19 18 17 16 15 14 13 12 11 10 9 8 7 6 5 4 3 2 1

Printed in Dubai by Oriental Press

A catalogue record for this publication is available from the British Library

ISBN 978-1-108-65910-9 Listening, Speaking and Critical Thinking Student's Book, Mobile App & Online Workbook 3 with Downloadable Audio & Video

CONTENTS

MAP OF THE BOOK

UNIT	VIDEO	LISTENING	VOCABULARY	
1 ANIMALS Listening 1: A debate about using animals for work (Biology / Zoology) Listening 2: A presentation about the human threats to polar bears (Biology / Zoology / Environmental science)	The mental skills of chimpanzees	**Key listening skills:** Taking notes Listening for contrasting ideas Listening for signposting language **Additional skills:** Understanding key vocabulary Using your knowledge Predicting content using visuals Listening for main ideas Listening for text organization Listening for detail Synthesizing **Pronunciation for listening:** Intonation of lists	Word families	
2 THE ENVIRONMENT Listening 1: A lecture about hydroponic agriculture (Ecology / Environmental science) Listening 2: A debate about nuclear power (Environmental science / Political science)	Blowing in the wind: offshore wind farms	**Key listening skills:** Listening for explanations Listening for counter-arguments **Additional skills:** Understanding key vocabulary Predicting content using visuals Using your knowledge Listening for main ideas Listening for detail Summarizing Listening for text organization Taking notes on main ideas Synthesizing **Pronunciation for listening:** Connected speech: linking sounds	Negative prefixes	
3 TRANSPORT Listening 1: A radio programme about the fear of flying (Psychology / Sociology) Listening 2: A presentation about cycling to work (Sociology / Civil engineering)	The air travel revolution	**Key listening skill:** Listening for rhetorical questions **Additional skills:** Understanding key vocabulary Using your knowledge Listening for main ideas Taking notes on detail Listening for detail Listening for text organization Synthesizing **Pronunciation for listening:** Word stress	Talking about problems and solutions	
4 CUSTOMS AND TRADITIONS Listening 1: A podcast about changing customs in the modern world (Anthropology / Cultural studies) Listening 2: A discussion about gift-giving (Sociology / Cultural studies)	Chinese moon cakes	**Key listening skills:** Identifying cause and effect Listening for opinion **Additional skills:** Understanding key vocabulary Using your knowledge Listening for main ideas Taking notes on detail Synthesizing **Pronunciation for listening:** Connected speech: /t/ and /d/ at the end of words	Suffixes	

GRAMMAR	CRITICAL THINKING	SPEAKING
Modals for obligation, prohibition and advice	Creating a talk for a specific audience	*Preparation for speaking:* Using signposting language Introducing examples Expressing general beliefs *Pronunciation for speaking:* Signposting phrases *Speaking task:* Give a two-minute presentation about the human threats to an endangered species.
Modal verbs to express future possibility	Making counter-arguments	*Preparation for speaking:* Linking ideas with transition words and phrases Talking about advantages and disadvantages Giving counter-arguments *Speaking task:* Take part in a debate about allowing a new wind farm near your town.
Comparative and superlative adjectives	Evaluating problems and proposing solutions	*Preparation for speaking:* Giving recommendations Expanding on an idea *Speaking task:* Give a presentation on a transport problem and suggest solutions to solve the problem.
Dependent prepositions	Creating a convincing argument	*Preparation for speaking:* Being polite in a discussion Using adverbs for emphasis Phrases with *that* *Pronunciation:* Stress patterns in phrases for agreeing and disagreeing *Speaking task:* Take part in a discussion about whether special occasions have become too commercial.

UNIT	VIDEO	LISTENING	VOCABULARY	
5 HEALTH AND FITNESS Listening 1: A podcast about why some people live a long life (Health Science) Listening 2: Four presentations about programmes to improve your health (taekwondo, team sports, cycling, acupuncture) (Health Science / Sports management)	Childhood obesity	**_Key listening skills:_** Listening for attitude Identifying references to common knowledge **_Additional skills_** Understanding key vocabulary Using your knowledge Listening for main ideas Taking notes on detail Synthesizing **_Pronunciation for listening:_** Attitude and emotion	Adjectives to describe well-being	
6 DISCOVERY AND INVENTION Listening 1: A museum tour about inventions from the Middle Ages (History) Listening 2: A lecture about the history of smartphone apps (Art and design)	A helping hand	**_Key listening skills:_** Understanding references to earlier ideas Understanding lecture organization **_Additional skills:_** Understanding key vocabulary Using your knowledge Listening for main ideas Taking notes on detail Listening for text organization Synthesizing **_Pronunciation for listening:_** Weak and strong forms	Uses of the verb *make*	
7 FASHION Listening 1: A discussion about clothes of the future (Fashion design / Business) Listening 2: An interview with a fashion designer (Fashion design / Business / Marketing)	Interview with College of Art graduate Christopher Raeburn	**_Key listening skills:_** Taking notes on main ideas and details Identifying auxiliary verbs for emphasis **_Additional skills:_** Understanding key vocabulary Predicting content using visuals Using your knowledge Listening for main ideas Making inferences Synthesizing **_Pronunciation for listening:_** Vowel omission	Idioms	
8 ECONOMICS Listening 1: A podcast about millionaire lifestyles (Sociology / Economics / Business) Listening 2: A discussion about whether university students should be paid for good grades (Sociology / Economics)	Workshops for entrepreneurs	**_Key listening skill:_** Understanding paraphrases **_Additional skills:_** Understanding key vocabulary Using your knowledge Listening for main ideas Taking notes on detail Listening for opinion Synthesizing **_Pronunciation for listening:_** Silent letters	Collocations with *pay* and *money*	

GRAMMAR	CRITICAL THINKING	SPEAKING
Phrasal verbs	Brainstorming and evaluating ideas using an ideas map	***Preparation for speaking:*** Problem–solution organization Presenting persuasively ***Speaking task:*** Give a presentation to a group of students about an idea for a health product or programme.
Passive verb forms	Summarizing information using *Wh-* questions	***Preparation for speaking:*** Previewing a topic Organizing ideas Explaining how something is used ***Speaking task:*** Give a presentation about an invention or discovery which has changed our lives.
Predictions and expectations about the future	Creating a purpose statement Evaluating interview questions	***Preparation for speaking:*** Asking for opinions and checking information Asking follow-up questions ***Speaking task:*** Take part in an interview to find out attitudes about uniforms and dress codes.
Conditional sentences	Evaluating arguments	***Preparation for speaking:*** Using gerunds as subjects to talk about actions Presenting reasons and evidence to support an argument Using paraphrases ***Speaking task:*** Take part in a discussion about whether young people should be allowed to have credit cards.

YOUR GUIDE TO UNLOCK

Unlock your academic potential

Unlock Second Edition is a six-level, academic-light English course created to build the skills and language students need for their studies (CEFR Pre-A1 to C1). It develops students' ability to think critically in an academic context right from the start of their language learning. Every level has 100% new inspiring video on a range of academic topics.

Confidence in teaching.
Joy in learning.

Better Learning WITH UNLOCK SECOND EDITION

Better Learning is our simple approach where insights we've gained from research have helped shape content that drives results. We've listened to teachers all around the world and made changes so that *Unlock* Second Edition better supports students along the way to academic success.

CRITICAL THINKING

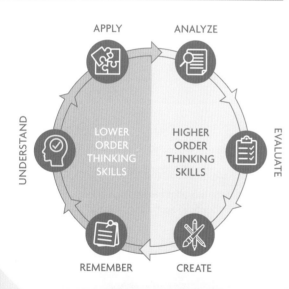

Critical thinking in *Unlock* Second Edition ...

- is **informed** by a range of academic research from Bloom in the 1950s, to Krathwohl and Anderson in the 2000s, to more recent considerations relating to 21st Century Skills
- has a **refined** syllabus with a better mix of higher- and lower-order critical thinking skills
- is **measurable**, with objectives and self-evaluation so students can track their critical thinking progress
- is **transparent** so teachers and students know when and why they're developing critical thinking skills
- is **supported** with professional development material for teachers so teachers can teach with confidence

... so that students have the best possible chance of academic success.

INSIGHT

Most classroom time is currently spent on developing lower-order critical thinking skills. Students need to be able to use higher-order critical thinking skills too.

CONTENT

Unlock Second Edition includes the right mix of lower- and higher-order thinking skills development in every unit, with clear learning objectives.

RESULTS

Students are better prepared for their academic studies and have the confidence to apply the critical thinking skills they have developed.

CLASSROOM APP

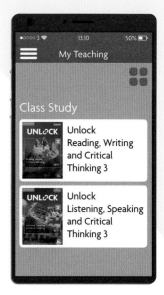

The *Unlock* Second Edition Classroom App ...

- offers extra, **motivating** practice in speaking, critical thinking and language
- provides a **convenient** bank of language and skills reference informed by our exclusive Corpus research ⊙
- is easily **accessible** and **navigable** from students' mobile phones
- is fully **integrated** into every unit
- provides Unlock-**specific** activities to extend the lesson whenever you see this symbol 📱PLUS

... so that students can easily get the right, extra practice they need, when they need it.

INSIGHT

The learning material on a Classroom app is most effective when it's an integral, well-timed part of a lesson.

CONTENT

Every unit of *Unlock* Second Edition is enhanced with bespoke Classroom app material to extend the skills and language students are learning in the book. The symbol 📱PLUS shows when to use the app.

RESULTS

Students are motivated by having relevant extension material on their mobile phones to maximize their language learning. Teachers are reassured that the Classroom App adds real language-learning value to their lessons.

RESEARCH

We have gained deeper insights to inform *Unlock* Second Edition by ...

- carrying out **extensive market research** with teachers and students to fully understand their needs throughout the course's development
- consulting **academic research** into critical thinking
- refining our vocabulary syllabus using our **exclusive Corpus research** ⊙

... so that you can be assured of the quality of *Unlock* Second Edition.

INSIGHT

- Consultation with global Advisory Panel
- Comprehensive reviews of material
- Face-to-face interviews and Skype™ calls
- Classroom observations

CONTENT

- Improved critical thinking
- 100% new video and video lessons
- Clearer contexts for language presentation and practice
- Text-by-text glossaries
- Online Workbooks with more robust content
- Comprehensive teacher support

RESULTS

"Thank you for all the effort you've put into developing Unlock Second Edition. As far as I can see, I think the new edition is more academic and more appealing to young adults."

Burçin Gönülsen,
Işık Üniversity, Turkey

HOW *UNLOCK* WORKS

Unlock your knowledge
Encourages discussion around the themes of the unit with inspiration from interesting questions and striking images.

UNLOCK YOUR KNOWLEDGE

Work with a partner. Discuss the questions.

1 What are the people in the photo doing?
2 Is fashion important to you? Why / Why not?
3 What do young people like to wear in your country at the moment?
4 Has fashion changed a lot in your country in the last 50 years? How has it changed?
5 What do you think are some reasons why fashions change?

Watch and listen
Features an engaging and motivating video which generates interest in the topic and develops listening skills.

WATCH AND LISTEN

ACTIVATING YOUR KNOWLEDGE

PREPARING TO WATCH

1 Work with a partner. Read the definitions in the box and discuss the questions below.

ethical brand (n phr) a product which is produced in a way that does not hurt anyone or anything, for example, without hurting animals or

LISTENING

Listening 1
Provides information about the topic and practises pre-listening, while-listening and post-listening skills. This section may also include a focus on pronunciation which will further enhance listening comprehension.

LISTENING

LISTENING 1

UNDERSTANDING KEY VOCABULARY

PREPARING TO LISTEN

1 You are going to listen to a discussion about clothes of the future. Before you listen, read the definitions. Complete the sentences with the words in bold.

convert (v) to change something into something else
design (n) the way in which something is arranged or shaped
fabric (n) cloth, material
focus on (phr v) to give a lot of attention to one subject or thing
local (adj) relating to an area nearby

Language development
Practises the vocabulary and grammar from Listening 1 and pre-teaches the vocabulary and grammar for Listening 2.

LANGUAGE DEVELOPMENT

IDIOMS

Idioms are expressions which are often used in spoken English. An idiom doesn't always have a meaning which can easily be understood from looking at its individual words. You need to look at the whole expression to understand it.
I **keep my eye on** the fashion trends in other countries.
(= watch something)
Try to memorize any new idioms and use them when you speak.

1 Complete the sentences with the idioms from the box.

Listening 2
Presents a second listening text on the topic, often in a different format, and serves as a model for the speaking task.

LISTENING 2

UNDERSTANDING KEY VOCABULARY

PREPARING TO LISTEN

1 You are going to listen to a radio interview. Before you listen, read the sentences (1–5) below and write the correct form of the words in bold next to the definitions (a–h).

1 Aysha's **collection** was presented during the last Fashion Week in Doha.
2 I have always tried to **combine** my culture with fashion.
3 As a teenager, I would make my own skirts and scarves. I wanted my designs to be **individual**. They were **unique** and, eventually, people **admired** my clothes rather than laughed at me.

SPEAKING

Critical thinking

Develops the lower- and higher-order thinking skills required for the speaking task.

Preparation for speaking

Presents and practises functional language, pronunciation and speaking strategies for the speaking task.

Speaking task

Uses the skills and language learned throughout the unit to support students in producing a presentational or interactional speaking task. This is the unit's main learning objective.

Objectives review

Allows learners to evaluate how well they have mastered the skills covered in the unit.

Wordlist

Lists the key vocabulary from the unit. The most frequent words used at this level in an academic context are highlighted.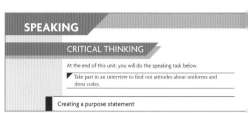

Unlock offers 56 hours per Student's Book, which is extendable to 90 hours with the Classroom App, Online Workbook and other additional activities in the Teacher's Manual and Development Pack.

Unlock is a paired-skills course with two separate Student's Books per level. For levels 1–5 (CEFR A1 – C1), these are **Reading, Writing and Critical Thinking** and **Listening, Speaking and Critical Thinking**. They share the same unit topics so you have access to a wide range of material at each level. Each Student's Book provides access to the Classroom App and Online Workbook.

Unlock Basic has been developed for pre-A1 learners. **Unlock Basic Skills** integrates reading, writing, listening, speaking and critical thinking in one book to provide students with an effective and manageable learning experience. **Unlock Basic Literacy** develops and builds confidence in literacy. The *Basic* books also share the same unit topics and so can be used together or separately, and **Unlock Basic Literacy** can be used for self-study.

Student components

Resource	Description	Access

Student's Books	• Levels 1–5 come with Classroom App, Online Workbook, and downloadable audio and video
	  – Levels 1–4 (8 units)
	  – Level 5 (10 units)
	• *Unlock Basic Skills* comes with downloadable audio and video (11 units)
	• *Unlock Basic Literacy* comes with downloadable audio (11 units)
		• The Classroom App and Online Workbook are on the **CLMS** and are accessed via the unique code inside the front cover of the Student's Book
		• The audio and video are downloadable from the Resources tab on the **CLMS**

Online Workbook	• Levels 1–5 only • Extension activities to further practise the language and skills learned • All-new vocabulary activities in the Online Workbooks practise the target vocabulary in new contexts	• The Online Workbook is on the **CLMS** and is accessed via the unique code inside the front cover of the Student's Book
Classroom App	• Levels 1–5 only • Extra practice in speaking, critical thinking and language	• The app is downloadable from the **Apple App Store** or **Google Play** • Students use the same login details as for the **CLMS**, and then they are logged in for a year
Video	• Levels 1–5 and *Unlock Basic Skills* only • All the video from the course	• The video is downloadable from the Resources tab on the **CLMS**
Audio	• All the audio from the course	• The audio is downloadable from the Resources tab on the **CLMS** and from **cambridge.org/unlock**

Teacher components

Resource	Description	Access
Teacher's Manual and Development Pack	• One manual covers Levels 1–5 • It contains flexible lesson plans, lesson objectives, additional activities and common learner errors as well as professional development for teachers, *Developing critical thinking skills in your students* • It comes with downloadable audio and video, vocabulary worksheets and peer-to-peer teacher training worksheets	• The audio, video and worksheets are downloadable from the Resources tab on the **CLMS** and from **eSource** via the code inside the front cover of the manual
Presentation Plus	• Software for interactive whiteboards so you can present the pages of the Student's Books and easily play audio and video, and check answers	• Please contact your sales rep for codes to download Presentation Plus from **eSource**

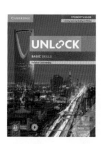
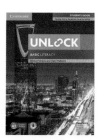

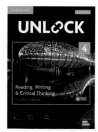

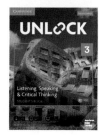
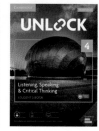

LEARNING OBJECTIVES	IN THIS UNIT YOU WILL ...
Watch and listen	watch and understand a video about the mental skills of chimpanzees.
Listening skills	take notes; listen for contrasting ideas; listen for signposting language.
Critical thinking	create a talk for a specific audience; organize information for a presentation.
Grammar	use modals for obligation, prohibition and advice.
Speaking skills	use signposting language; introduce examples; express general beliefs.
Speaking task	give a two-minute presentation about the human threats to an endangered species.

UNLOCK YOUR KNOWLEDGE

Work with a partner. Discuss the questions.

1 Look at the photo. What work are the animals doing?

2 Do people use animals for work in your country? If yes, what work do they do?

3 What other types of work can animals do?

PLUS

WATCH AND LISTEN

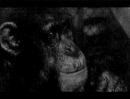

‹ ›

PREPARING TO WATCH

ACTIVATING YOUR KNOWLEDGE

1 Work with a partner. Discuss the questions.

1 Can animals solve problems? Give examples.
2 How do animals play? Do you think they like puzzles or games? Why / Why not?

PREDICTING CONTENT USING VISUALS

2 Work with a partner. Look at the photos from the video and discuss the questions.

1 What is the goal of a game like a maze?
2 In your opinion, is the chimpanzee thinking? Why / Why not?
3 Do you think the chimpanzee and the man are happy or angry? Explain your answer.

GLOSSARY

mental (adj) relating to the mind

maze (n) a type of puzzle with a series of paths from entrance to exit

in the wild (phr) in nature, not in a zoo, on a farm or as a pet

reflect upon (phr v) to think about in a serious and careful way

WHILE WATCHING

UNDERSTANDING MAIN IDEAS

3 ▶ Watch the video. Circle the correct answers.

1 The scientists wanted to find out if chimpanzees could _____ .
   a look for food
   b plan ahead
   c protect themselves
2 The chimpanzee is able to _____ .
   a use a computer
   b ask for food
   c listen to commands

3 The goal of the game is to _____ .
   a climb the stairs
   b eat the cherries
   c find the exit
4 Sometimes Panzee, the chimpanzee, is able to solve a maze more quickly than _____ can.
   a a human
   b a computer
   c the scientist
5 According to the professor, chimpanzees are able to _____ .
   a communicate
   b make plans
   c think faster than people

4 ▶ Watch the video again. Write *T* (true), *F* (false) or *DNS* (does not say) next to the statements. Then, correct the false statements.

_____ 1 In the wild, chimpanzees have to look for friends.
_____

_____ 2 Panzee can often complete mazes which she has never seen before.
_____

_____ 3 Planning before acting is just a human skill.
_____

_____ 4 The scientist says that chimpanzees reflect upon the past.
_____

_____ 5 Chimpanzees can plan ahead for centuries.
_____

DISCUSSION

5 Work in small groups. Discuss the questions. Then, compare your answers with another group.
   1 Make a list of five animals which are very intelligent.
   2 For each animal you chose, give an example of its intelligence.
   3 Do you think animals remember things? Give reasons and examples for your answer.

LISTENING

LISTENING 1

PREPARING TO LISTEN

1 You are going to listen to a debate about using animals for work. Before you listen, read the definitions. Complete the sentences with the words in bold.

> **abuse** (n) violent or unfair treatment of someone
> **conditions** (n pl) the situation in which someone lives or works
> **cruel** (adj) not kind
> **issue** (n) a topic or problem which causes concern and discussion
> **protect** (v) to keep safe from danger
> **suffer** (v) to feel pain or unhappiness
> **survive** (v) to continue to live, in spite of danger and difficulty
> **welfare** (n) someone's or something's health and happiness

1 Some people feel that using elephants in the circus is animal _____ . To be healthy, elephants need to live in the wild.
2 This animal organization helps to _____ animals which are in danger. It saves thousands of animals every year.
3 People who let animals go hungry are _____ . I don't understand how they can do that.
4 Some wild animals _____ in zoos. They live in small, uncomfortable cages and they don't have enough space to run.
5 The _____ in this zoo are excellent. All of the animals have plenty of space and are treated very well.
6 The biggest _____ for many animal rights organizations is the use of animals in scientific experiments.
7 Sharks continue to _____ in the ocean, despite the threat from humans.
8 There are laws which protect the _____ of animals by making sure humans are punished for hurting them.

2 Work with a partner. Discuss the questions.

1 What are some reasons in favour of using animals for work?
2 What are some reasons against using animals for work?
3 What is your opinion about using animals for work?

3 🔊 1.1 Listen to the debate and check your answers for questions 1–2.

WHILE LISTENING

4 🔊 1.1 Listen to the debate again and complete the table. What are the animals used for?

	protection	building	transport	war
dogs	✔			
horses				
elephants				
camels				

Taking notes

Taking notes while listening will make you a more active listener. There are many ways to take notes while listening. One way to take notes is by using a T-chart. T-charts can help you organize information into two aspects of a topic, such as pros and cons, or facts and opinions.

Using Animals for Work

cons (against)	pros (for)
cruel	helps poor people

5 🔊 1.1 Listen to the debate again. What are Ms Johnson's and Dr Kuryan's opinions on using animals for work? Complete the student's notes in the T-chart using words from the box.

| cruel   poor   rights   skills   survive   ~~technology~~ |

cons (Ms Johnson's ideas)	pros (Dr Kuryan's ideas)
1 We have <u>technology</u> which can replace animals.	4 Humans don't have the _____ or strength to do certain jobs.
2 Animals have no one to represent them and protect their _____ .	5 _____ people still need animals to survive.
3 Using animals for work is old-fashioned and _____ .	6 Domesticated animals wouldn't have been able to _____ without humans.

POST-LISTENING

Listening for contrasting ideas

Speakers use certain words and phrases to signal a contrast, or difference, between two ideas. To identify contrasting ideas, listen for these transition words and phrases: *yet, but, on the contrary, even though, however.*

Animals, like elephants and horses, were used to build amazing structures, like the pyramids in Egypt. **Yet/But** their hard work and suffering are hardly ever recognized.

Not all animal use is abuse. **On the contrary**, without humans, these domesticated animals would not have been able to survive.

Even though animals work hard for us, they are often abandoned when they get sick or too old to work.

These animals work long hours and live in difficult conditions. **However**, they get very little reward.

LISTENING FOR TEXT
ORGANIZATION

6 Circle the correct contrasting transition words and phrases. Use the examples in the box above to help you.

1 *Even though / However* I love animals, I don't think people should keep them in their homes.

2 Some people think the reason I became a vegetarian is because I love animals. *Even though / On the contrary*, I am a vegetarian for health reasons and not because I care about animal rights.

3 Many people are against animal testing. *Even though / Yet* without such tests, we would not have developed new medicines.

4 *Even though / Yet* people claim that animal rights aren't protected, there are many organizations which focus on this issue.

5 Many people eat meat. *Yet / On the contrary*, humans don't need animal protein to stay healthy.

7 Complete the extracts with the transition words and phrases in the box. Sometimes more than one answer is possible.

> but   even though   however   on the contrary   yet

1 People talk a lot about protecting animals, _____ they often don't do anything to help the animals.
2 Zoos are fun places for children to visit. _____ , some zoos do not provide good living conditions for their animals.
3 _____ I like animals, I wouldn't want to be a vet.
4 Most people aren't cruel to animals. _____ , they care a lot about animal welfare.

DISCUSSION

8 Read the statements. Do you agree or disagree with them? Work alone and make notes. Think of reasons for your opinion.

1 In the modern world, there is no longer any need to use animals for work. We have developed technology which can replace them. Using animals for work is similar to using children to work in factories.
2 People often spend too much time and money on animals. They should focus less on helping animals and more on helping poor people.

9 Work in a group of three. Discuss your opinions.

⊙ LANGUAGE DEVELOPMENT

WORD FAMILIES

VOCABULARY

You can develop your academic vocabulary by learning about word families. Word families often start the same and end differently, depending on the form (noun, verb, adjective or adverb). When you write down a new word, make sure to write down any other forms from its word family. If you don't know a word, you may be able to guess it from another form of the word.

1 Complete the table. In some items, more than one answer is possible. Use a dictionary to help you.

noun	verb	adjective	adverb
abandonment			
	abuse		abusively
analysis	analyze	analytical	analytically
communication			communicatively
	connect		
		damaged	
	debate		
environment			
		involved	
protection			protectively
	support		supportively
survivor / survival			

2 Complete the sentences with the correct form of the words in brackets.

1 The _____analysis_____ of the blood sample showed that the horse was healthy. (analyze)
2 Domesticated animals may find it very hard to _____ in the wild. (survive)
3 Owners sometimes _____ their animals on the street when they can no longer care for them. (abandon)
4 She is a strong _____ of animal rights. (support)
5 Using _____ damaging chemicals on farms can endanger wild animals as well as plants. (environment)

6 Some scientists have explored how birds _____ with each other by using different sounds. (communicate)

7 She has had a lot of _____ with animal rights for the last 25 years. (involve)

8 Many people are very _____ towards animals and they want to care for them. (protect)

9 I listened to a _____ about animal rights. (debate)

10 Many people who are _____ to animals aren't that way on purpose. (abuse)

MODALS FOR OBLIGATION, PROHIBITION AND ADVICE

Use *have to, have got to, need to* or *must* before a verb to say that something is an obligation. In other words, that it is necessary.

Animals **have to / have got to / need to / must** find food, water and a safe place to live in order to survive.

Use *don't have to* or *don't need to* to say that something is not an obligation.

You **don't have to / don't need to** feed the chickens. I've already fed them.

Use *mustn't* to say that something is prohibited, or not allowed.

Visitors to the zoo **mustn't** touch the animals.

Use *should* or *ought to* to give advice that you are sure about.

You **should / ought to** give some money to that animal rights organization. It does good work.

Use *might* or *could* to give advice when you are not sure.

It **might** be a good idea to volunteer at the animal shelter.

You **could** volunteer at the animal shelter.

3 Look at the sentences and the underlined modals. What does each sentence express? Write *O* (obligation), *P* (prohibition) or *A* (advice) next to each sentence.

1 You <u>have to</u> love animals to be a vet. _____

2 You <u>mustn't</u> give human food to animals. _____

3 If you want to work with animals, you <u>could</u> become a vet. _____

4 We <u>must</u> do more as a society to prevent animal cruelty. _____

5 What courses do you <u>need to</u> complete to get a veterinary degree? _____

6 You <u>ought to</u> visit the San Diego Zoo. It has some great animals. _____

7 We <u>should</u> be kind to animals. They have feelings, too. _____

8 It <u>might</u> be a good idea to help out on a farm if you are interested in working with animals. _____

4 Circle the sentence which best matches each picture.

1 a We have to wear a uniform.
  b We shouldn't wear a uniform.

2 a You mustn't park here.
  b You don't have to park here.

3 a You've got to buy a ticket.
  b You don't need to buy a ticket.

4 a He shouldn't wear this to work.
  b He doesn't need to wear this to work.

PLUS

PREPARING TO LISTEN

UNDERSTANDING KEY VOCABULARY

1 You are going to listen to a presentation about human threats to polar bears. Before you listen, read the sentences and circle the best definition for the word or phrase in bold.

1 Climate change is causing ice in the oceans to **melt**.
   a to become liquid as a result of heating
   b to get colder and become solid

2 Some species of bat are in danger because farmers spray plants, their biggest food **source**, with dangerous chemicals.
   a the cause of something
   b where something comes from

3 Polar bears are **endangered**. If we don't do something to save them, they will probably disappear.
   a at risk of no longer existing
   b very dangerous to humans

4 Most people have only seen lions in a zoo or animal park and not in their own **habitat** in the African savannah.
   a the natural environment of an animal or plant
   b a building where animals live when they are kept in a zoo

5 There are two **species** of elephants: Asian elephants and African elephants.
   a a type of animal which is under threat
   b a group of plants or animals which share similar features

6 Polar bears **depend on** sea ice for survival. Without the ice, it's difficult for them to hunt for seals.
   a to need
   b to have

7 Oil spills can **damage** the polar bear's environment and can even kill them.
   a to hurt
   b to help

8 The single greatest human **threat** to the environment is climate change.
   a the possibility of trouble, danger or disaster
   b a suggestion for improvement

2 Work with a partner. Check your answers to Exercise 1.

3 Look at the photos and answer the questions.

  1 Can you explain what is happening in the photos?
  2 What threats do you think the speaker will talk about?
  3 Can you think of any other threats to polar bears?

4 🔊 1.2 Listen to the presentation. Were your ideas mentioned?

WHILE LISTENING

5 🔊 1.2 Listen to the presentation again and complete the notes.

human threats to polar bears	what people are doing to help polar bears
1 loss of sea ice habitat	4
2	5
3	6

6 🔊 1.2 Complete the sentences. Then, listen again to check your answers.

  1 There are only about _____ polar bears in the world today.
  2 Most polar bears will probably be gone by _____ if nothing changes.
  3 The disappearing ice has several _____ effects.
  4 When polar bears go near _____ , people sometimes kill the bears to protect themselves.
  5 Groups are creating plans to make Arctic shipping _____ .
  6 To help save polar bears, you should use less electricity and _____ .

POST-LISTENING

LISTENING FOR TEXT ORGANIZATION

> **SKILLS**
>
> ## Listening for signposting language
>
> When you listen to a presentation, listen for signposting phrases (*first, second, to summarize*). These phrases are like road signs – they help you know when a speaker is moving to a new point or section.
>
> **First,** overfishing of the coastal waters has reduced the seabirds' food supply.
>
> **Second,** habitat destruction has reduced the amount of land on which the birds can nest.
>
> **To summarize,** the actions of people are pushing the local seabird population towards extinction.

7 🔊 1.3 Listen to extracts from the presentation and write the signposting phrases you hear.

1 _____ , Arctic communities are trying to reduce contact between humans and polar bears.

2 _____ , governments have made laws which limit the amount of oil production in the Arctic.

3 So, _____ , the main threat to polar bears is loss of habitat due to climate change.

PRONUNCIATION FOR LISTENING

> **SKILLS**
>
> ## Intonation of lists
>
> Speakers often list examples of what they are talking about. Giving a list of examples can help persuade the audience. These lists have their own intonation patterns. Speakers pause between each example in the list and stress each word.
>
> If the list is complete, the last example in the list has falling intonation, like this:
>
> 🔊 1.4 ... <u>beautiful</u> ↗, <u>powerful</u> ↗, <u>majestic</u> ↘
>
> If the list is not complete, the last example has rising intonation, like this:
>
> 🔊 1.5 ... warmer <u>temperatures</u> ↗, <u>floods</u> ↗, <u>droughts</u> ↗, huge <u>storms</u> ... ↗
>
> When you are taking notes, it is important to listen for this intonation so you know that the list isn't complete yet.

8 🔊 1.6 Listen to the lists. Is each list complete or not complete? Tick the correct answer.

	complete	not complete
1 large, white, strong		
2 pandas, sea turtles, chimpanzees, tigers		
3 human contact, climate change, industrial development		
4 more lights, electric fences, warning plans		

9 🔊 1.6 Listen to the lists again. Practise saying each list with rising and falling intonation.

DISCUSSION

SYNTHESIZING

10 Work in small groups. Use ideas from Listening 1 and Listening 2 to answer the following questions.

1 Do you think humans should be responsible for protecting animals? Why / Why not?

2 There are about 8.7 million species on Earth. Does it matter if some of them become extinct? Why / Why not?

SPEAKING

CRITICAL THINKING

At the end of this unit, you are going to do the speaking task below.

> Give a two-minute presentation about the human threats to an endangered species.

Creating a talk for a specific audience

When you are preparing to give a presentation, it is important to think about who your audience will be. If the audience is already familiar with the topic, you may not need to explain certain ideas. However, if the audience does not know much about the topic, you will need to explain your ideas so they understand what you are talking about. You will also need to use language of an appropriate level for the audience.

ANALYZE

1 Read the introductions to three different talks about polar bears. Who is the audience for each talk? Write A (young children), B (secondary-school students) or C (scientists).

1 Today, I'm going to talk about the human threats to polar bears. Most of these threats are caused by climate change. First, can anyone tell me some of the effects of climate change?
Audience: _____

2 Today, we're going to review the latest research regarding the substantial impacts of human activity on the habitat of the polar bear and discuss ways in which technological innovations can contribute to reducing these threats.
Audience: _____

3 Today, I'm going to tell you all about polar bears. Polar bears are very big bears. They live in cold places. Put your hand up if you know what colour polar bears are.
Audience: _____

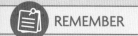

2 Think about Listening 2 and circle the correct answer.

1 Who is the audience? Who is the speaker talking to?
   a scientists
   b university students
   c work colleagues

2 What is the speaker's most important objective or purpose?
   a to inform the audience about human threats to the polar bear
   b to teach the audience about polar bears' habits
   c to explain about the effects of climate change

3 The speaker in Listening 2 used this table to plan her presentation. Complete the table. Use information from your notes on page 26.

main idea	_____ are threatened by humans.
supporting details	Threats: • • • What people are doing to help: • • •
conclusion / summary	

4 Choose an endangered species to talk about. Use one of the species in the box or choose another. Decide who your audience will be (young children / secondary school students / people at a professional conference / people in your community). Complete the planning table for your presentation. You can do an internet search for information.

| gorilla | rhino | sea turtle | tiger | whale |

Audience: _____

Objective: _____

main idea	
supporting details	Threats: • • • What people are doing to help: • • •
conclusion / summary	

5 Look at your notes in the planning table. Imagine you are doing a presentation on the same topic for a different audience. What changes would you make to your presentation? Share your ideas with a partner.

EVALUATE

SIGNPOSTING A PRESENTATION

1 🔊 1.7 Listen to a presentation about using animals for entertainment. Answer the questions.

1 What is the speaker's opinion about using animals for entertainment?

_____

2 What points does the speaker make?

_____

_____

_____

3 What examples does the speaker give to support each point?

_____

_____

_____

4 What advice does the speaker give at the end of the presentation?

_____

_____

Using signposting language

Use signposting phrases to help your audience follow your presentation.

To introduce the first point

First,
First of all,

To add another idea

Furthermore,
Second,
Another point is that ...
Finally,

To introduce a conclusion

To sum up,
In conclusion,
To summarize,
In short,

2 Choose the correct signposting phrase for each sentence.

1 _____ , I'd like to remind you that you can make a difference. Thank you so much for coming today. You've been a great audience!
   a Another point is that   b First of all   c To conclude

2 There are several issues with producing oil in the Arctic. First, it's expensive. _____ , it's bad for the environment.
   a In short   b Furthermore   c To summarize

3 Today I'm going to talk about endangered species and what we can do to help them. _____ , we can give money to environmental organizations.
   a First   b To sum up   c Second

Introducing examples

Speakers also use signposting phrases (*for instance, for example, such as*) to introduce examples.

Another point is that zoos have an important educational role. **For instance**, children can see animals up close.
Keeping animals in zoos helps protect them. **For example**, many species, **such as** the giant panda and the snow leopard, are endangered.

3 Work with a partner. Add your own examples to these points.

1 I think that zoos are sometimes good for animals. For example, _____
_____ .

2 You can see many exotic animals in zoos, such as _____
_____ .

3 Animals are sometimes unhappy in zoos. For instance, _____
_____ .

Expressing general beliefs

In a presentation, use phrases like *It's believed that* … to talk about what most people think or believe. This shows that the idea is not only your idea.

It's often said that it's cruel to use animals for entertainment.
It's believed that most of the polar bears will be gone by 2050 if nothing changes.
It's widely known that climate change is a threat to polar bears.

4 Work with a partner. Complete the sentences with your own ideas.

1 It's often said that _____ .
2 It's believed that _____ .
3 It's widely known that _____ .

PRONUNCIATION FOR SPEAKING

5 🔊 1.8 Listen to the extracts. Notice how the signposting phrases in bold are pronounced as one complete phrase. Underline the stressed word in each signposting phrase.

1 **First of all**, keeping animals in zoos helps protect them.
2 **For example**, many species, such as the giant panda and the snow leopard, are endangered in the wild.
3 **Another point is that** zoos have an important educational role.
4 **To summarize**, zoos help protect animals and educate us.
5 **In short**, modern zoos are comfortable, safe places for wild animals.

6 🔊 1.8 Listen to the extracts again and practise saying the sentences.

SPEAKING TASK

▶ Give a two-minute presentation about the human threats to an endangered species.

PREPARE

1 Look at the presentation plan you created in Exercise 4 in the Critical thinking section. Review your notes and add any new information.

2 Refer to the Task checklist below as you prepare your presentation.

3 Prepare some notes about your introduction.

4 For each supporting detail in your plan, make notes about the language you will use.

5 Prepare a concluding statement. Say what people should do to save the species.

TASK CHECKLIST	✔
Use transition words and phrases to contrast ideas.	
Use modals for obligation, prohibition and advice.	
Use appropriate intonation in lists.	
Support your points with examples.	
Use appropriate signposting language.	

PRACTISE

6 Work in a group of three. Take turns practising your presentations. Then, discuss the questions below. Take notes during the discussion.

1 Did the speaker clearly identify each threat to the species?
2 Did the speaker use signposting phrases to help the listener?
3 Did the speaker use examples to support points?
4 How could the speaker improve the presentation?

PRESENT

7 Take turns giving your presentations to the class.

OBJECTIVES REVIEW

1 Check your learning objectives for this unit. Write *3*, *2* or *1* for each objective.

3 = very well   2 = well   1 = not so well

I can ...

watch and understand a video about the mental skills
of chimpanzees.   _____

take notes.   _____

listen for contrasting ideas.   _____

listen for signposting language.   _____

create a talk for a specific audience.   _____

organize information for a presentation.   _____

use modals for obligation, prohibition and advice.   _____

use signposting language.   _____

introduce examples.   _____

express general beliefs.   _____

give a two-minute presentation about the human threats to
an endangered species.   _____

2 Go to the *Unlock* Online Workbook for more practice with this unit's
learning objectives.

UNLOCK ONLINE

WORDLIST

abandon (v) ☉	debate (v) ☉	source (n) ☉
abuse (n) ☉	depend on (phr v)	species (n) ☉
abuse (v) ☉	endangered (adj)	suffer (v) ☉
analyze (v) ☉	environment (n) ☉	support (v) ☉
communicate (v) ☉	habitat (n) ☉	survive (v) ☉
conditions (n pl) ☉	involve (v) ☉	threat (n) ☉
connect (v) ☉	issue (n) ☉	welfare (n)
cruel (adj)	melt (v)	
damage (v) ☉	protect (v) ☉	

☉ = high-frequency words in the Cambridge Academic Corpus

Watch and listen	watch and understand a video about offshore wind farms.
Listening skills	listen for explanations; listen for counter-arguments.
Critical thinking	make counter-arguments.
Grammar	use modals to express future possibility.
Speaking skills	link ideas with transition words and phrases; talk about advantages and disadvantages; give counter-arguments.
Speaking task	take part in a debate about allowing a new wind farm near your town.

THE ENVIRONMENT

UNIT 2

UNL⟳CK YOUR KNOWLEDGE

Work with a partner. Discuss the questions.

1 Look at the photo of solar panels. What do you know about this energy source?

2 What are some other sources of energy?

3 Are these energy sources common in your country? If not, what sources are common? Why?

4 What are the pros and cons of these sources of energy?

PLUS

PREPARING TO WATCH

ACTIVATING YOUR KNOWLEDGE

1 Work with a partner. Discuss the questions.

1 Why do people build wind turbines?

2 Have you ever seen wind turbines? Where? Describe them.

PREDICTING CONTENT USING VISUALS

2 Work with a partner. Look at the photos from the video. Discuss the questions.

1 How big do you think wind turbines are? Compare them to a building you know.

2 Why would people put a wind turbine in the ocean?

3 Why might a ship have 'legs'?

GLOSSARY

run out (phr v) to use all of something so that there is none left

alternative energy (n phr) power which comes from natural resources, like the sun or wind

turbine (n) a type of machine which uses air or water to produce power

assemble (v) to build something by putting parts together

WHILE WATCHING

3 ▶ Watch the video. Write *T* (true) or *F* (false) next to the statements. Then, correct the false statements.

1 People are using wind as a source of energy these days.

_____

_____ 2 The ship made it possible to build the turbines in the middle of London.

_____

_____ 3 The turbines can get energy even from light winds.

_____

_____ 4 It was difficult to build the turbines in sunny weather.

_____

_____ 5 One turbine can provide energy for thousands of homes.

_____

UNDERSTANDING MAIN IDEAS

4 ▶ Watch the video again. Complete the sentences with the numbers in the box.

12   120   175   3,000   500,000

1 The wind farm is about _____ miles from the coast of England.
2 There are _____ turbines in the London Array.
3 Each of the turbines is about _____ m across.
4 Each turbine can provide electricity for _____ homes.
5 The London Array provides electricity to more than _____ homes.

UNDERSTANDING DETAIL

DISCUSSION

5 Work with a partner. Discuss the questions.

1 Do you agree or disagree with the following statement?
   The government of my country should build more sources of alternative energy, like wind turbines.
   Give reasons and examples for your answer.
2 What could you do in your home to use less energy?

LISTENING

LISTENING 1

PREPARING TO LISTEN

1 You are going to listen to a lecture. Before you listen, circle the best definition for the word in bold.

1 Fossil fuels are a **limited** source of energy. Some scientists predict that they will be gone by the end of this century.
   a expensive to produce
   b small in amount or number
   c causing pollution of the planet

2 Wind can **provide** people with energy which is cheap and clean.
   a to give something
   b to make something
   c to depend on something

3 One **solution** to the problem of climate change is to use public transport.
   a a result of something
   b a way of solving a problem
   c a connection to something

4 We should use fewer fossil fuels and more **alternative** forms of energy, such as solar and wind power.
   a cleaner
   b less expensive
   c different

5 Climate change is the world's biggest **environmental** issue. If we don't do something about it, it will have terrible effects on the planet.
   a relating to the weather
   b relating to the air, water and land
   c relating to towns and cities

6 Scientists have developed a new **system** for growing food. It involves using solar energy to grow food in the desert.
   a a new or original idea
   b a farm where crops are grown
   c a way of doing things

7 Water is the world's most important **resource**, so it's important to protect it.
   a something you have and can use
   b a body of water, such as a lake or ocean
   c a kind of energy

8 It hasn't rained for six months, so our area is experiencing a water **crisis**.
   a a plan to fix something
   b a very dangerous or difficult situation
   c an organization

2 Work in a group of three. Look at the pictures and answer the questions.

1 What do you think will be the topic of the lecture?

_____

2 What do you think is happening in the pictures?

_____

3 What sources of energy are used on this farm?

_____

PRONUNCIATION FOR LISTENING

Connected speech: linking sounds

When people speak fluently, there is often an extra linking sound between words when the first word ends with a vowel sound and the second word starts with a vowel sound. Common linking sounds are /j/ and /w/.

This type of farming could solve some of the environmental problems we ⌣/j/⌣ are now facing.
The rest of the heated water goes to ⌣/w/⌣ a desalination plant.

3 🔊 2.1 Listen to the sentences. What linking sound do you hear between the words in bold? Write *j* or *w* next to each sentence.

1 Today I want **to explain** some alternative solutions. _____

2 As **we all** know, in order to grow plants we need water and sunlight. _____

3 I think that desert farms might **be a** very interesting way to farm in the future. _____

4 If **you add** the nutrients to water, you can grow fruit and vegetables in water. _____

WHILE LISTENING

LISTENING FOR
MAIN IDEAS

4 🔊 **2.2** Listen to the lecture and choose the best answers.

1 Desert farming uses solar energy and *water / traditional farming*.

2 NASA has been researching hydroponics because it allows us to grow food *with more water / in extreme climates*.

3 The greenhouse is heated by using *fresh water / solar power*.

4 The plants grow in a *greenhouse / desalination plant*.

5 Food from desert farms contains *no pesticides / more salt*.

6 People in *Australia / around the world* are excited about hydroponics.

7 Desert farms *use fossil fuels / can help solve the global food problem*.

8 The future of hydroponics is *known / not known*.

LISTENING FOR
DETAIL

5 🔊 **2.3** Listen to part of the lecture. Number the pictures (a–f) in the order you hear them (1–6).

HYDROPONICS PROCESS

a seawater in special containers

b a desalination plant

c tomatoes on sale in the supermarket

d mirrors for reflecting heat

e plants growing in the greenhouse

f pipe with hot oil inside

6 🔊 2.3 Listen again to part of the lecture and complete the summary.

Sundrop Farm, Australia: Hydroponics process

- The farm is (1)_____ metres from the sea.

- Heat is reflected from the (2)_____ onto a pipe which has oil inside.

- The hot oil heats up the (3)_____ .

- When the seawater is at a temperature of (4)_____ °C, the steam heats the greenhouse.

- The desalination plant produces up to (5)_____ litres of fresh water every day.

- No pesticides are used during the process.

- This type of farming has a minimal effect on the (6)_____ .

POST-LISTENING

Listening for explanations

In a lecture, speakers often explain difficult or new words. They do this by using certain phrases (e.g. *this means*) or by saying the same word in a simpler way.

Hydroponics means *growing plants in water.*

LISTENING FOR TEXT ORGANIZATION

7 Match the extracts from the lecture to the ways of explaining difficult or new words.

1 Scientists have combined solar energy with a farming technology called hydroponics. **Hydroponics means growing plants in water.** _____
2 ... they do need nutrients to help them grow. **Nutrients are like food for the plants.** _____
3 The rest of the heated water goes to a desalination plant. **Desalination is when we remove the salt from seawater to create drinkable water.** _____
4 Many supermarkets are interested in buying these vegetables because they're grown without pesticides **or other chemicals.** _____

The lecturer ...
a gives a simple example of what these things are similar to.
b says what group of things this belongs to.
c gives a simple explanation of a process.
d explains what the word means.

DISCUSSION

8 Work in small groups. Discuss the questions.

1 Do you know how the food you eat is grown? Is this important to you? Why / Why not?
2 Would you mind paying a lot more money for food if you knew it was produced in an environmentally friendly way? Why / Why not?
3 What do you think might be some problems with hydroponics?

NEGATIVE PREFIXES

1 A prefix is a group of letters which goes at the start of a word to make a new word with a different meaning. All the prefixes in the table below mean *not*. Match the words in the box to the prefixes in the table and write the word with its prefix. Use a dictionary to help you.

advantage   ~~necessary~~   correct
responsible   possible

prefix	example
un-	unnecessary
in-	
ir-	
dis-	
im-	

2 Write the correct prefix to complete the words.

1 Using nuclear power is _____responsible. It's just too dangerous.

2 Of course, the future of hydroponics is _____known. But I think it's going to become very common.

3 I _____agree that nuclear power is the best kind of energy. Solar power is much safer.

4 Solar power is cheap, clean and _____expensive. It costs much less than fossil fuels.

5 We are _____able to feed the world's population by traditional farming methods alone. Many people don't have enough food.

6 I don't think it's _____possible to end world hunger. Hydroponic farming could help.

7 That information is _____correct. Would you like me to give you the right information?

8 One _____advantage of wind power is that some people think the wind turbines are ugly.

9 Solar power is cheap, clean and _____limited. There will always be enough of it.

10 I _____approve of using chemicals to grow food. It's bad for the environment and it's bad for people's health.

PLUS

MODAL VERBS TO EXPRESS FUTURE POSSIBILITY

GRAMMAR

Use *will* (or *won't*) to say that you are certain about the future.

If there is an accident, then it **will** be huge and it **will** have long-term effects on the environment.

Use *could*, *might* or *may* to say that you are uncertain about the future. We'll briefly discuss how this type of farming **could/might/may** solve some of the environmental problems we are now facing.

Might is more common than *may* in conversation. *May* sounds more formal.

PLUS

3 🔊 2.4 Listen and complete these extracts from the lecture.

1 Today I want to explain some alternative solutions which _____ help reduce some of the problems related to climate change.

2 NASA scientists have been developing this method of growing food because it _____ allow us to grow food in any climate.

3 I think that desert farms _____ be a very interesting way to farm in the future.

4 Write the correct modal verb in the correct place in the sentences. You may also need to change the main verb. In some items, more than one answer is possible.

1 Farming in the desert solves the problem of food crisis. (uncertainty in the future)
   Farming in the desert **might** solve the problem of food crisis.

2 Not using fossil fuels reduces climate change. (uncertainty in the future)
   _____

3 Taxing fossil fuels reduces the use of cars. (certainty in the future)
   _____

4 Using solar energy does not lead to any environmental disasters. (certainty in the future)
   _____

5 Look again at the statements in Exercise 4. Do you agree or disagree with them? Discuss your opinions with a partner.

PREPARING TO LISTEN

1 You are going to listen to a debate about nuclear power. Before you listen, read the information about wind power. Complete the definitions with the correct form of the words in bold from the text.

Many people think wind power has a lot of **benefits**. First, it's very clean and it doesn't **pollute** the environment. Also, there are very few **risks** connected to wind power. Unlike coal mines and nuclear power plants, it is unlikely to cause accidents and it never leads to **disasters**. Most importantly, this source of energy is **affordable**. It's much cheaper than fossil fuels. However, not everyone thinks that wind power is a good idea. **Opponents** of wind power argue that the wind turbines can have a negative effect on the environment, and that turbines take up a lot of space. Opponents also say that the wind turbines aren't a **long-term** source of energy because, unlike nuclear power plants, the turbines need to be replaced after 10–15 years.

1 _____ (n) advantages
2 _____ (n) the possibility of something bad happening
3 _____ (adj) continuing for a long time
4 _____ (n) terrible accidents which cause a lot of damage
5 _____ (adj) not expensive
6 _____ (n) someone who disagrees with an idea
7 _____ (v) to make something, like air or water, dirty or harmful

PLUS

2 Work in small groups. What are the advantages and disadvantages of nuclear power? Write your ideas in the table.

advantages	disadvantages

3 🔊 2.5 Listen to the debate about nuclear power. Do the speakers mention any of the ideas which you listed in Exercise 2? Underline them in the table above.

WHILE LISTENING

4 🔊 2.5 Listen to the debate again. Are Emma and Jack for or against nuclear energy? What are some of the reasons they give? Take notes.

Emma

For or against?:

Reasons:

Jack

For or against?:

Reasons:

5 🔊 2.5 Listen to the debate again and circle the correct answers.

1 What are the two reasons why Emma mentions the Fukushima nuclear power plant?
   a To say that nuclear power plants can be dangerous.
   b To show that nuclear energy can help develop a country.
   c To give an example of the long-term effects of a nuclear disaster.
   d To show that nuclear power is usually safe.

2 What three arguments are mentioned in favour of nuclear energy?
   a It's cheap.
   b It doesn't pollute the air.
   c It uses advanced technology.
   d It can supply a lot of electricity for a long time.

3 What are two ways that nuclear energy can help developing countries?
   a They can export the energy.
   b They can buy the energy.
   c They can develop new technology.
   d They can be independent of gas and oil prices.

POST-LISTENING

SKILLS

Listening for counter-arguments

In a debate or a discussion, speakers often use counter-arguments to say why they disagree with a viewpoint. Speakers sometimes introduce a counter-argument with words or phrases like *and yet* or *but*.

Some people think that nuclear power is an environmentally friendly source of energy because it creates less pollution than traditional power plants. **But** opponents of nuclear energy believe that it has more dangers than benefits.

6 Read these extracts from the debate. What idea is the speaker arguing *against* in each extract?

1 Some people are worried that nuclear power is a big risk. **And yet,** there are hundreds of nuclear power plants all over the world and there have only been three major nuclear accidents in the last 30 years.
The speaker is arguing against the idea that _____
_____ .

2 Some people say that nuclear energy doesn't pollute the air, **but that's not completely true**. It takes many years to build a nuclear power plant. During this time, hundreds of machines work day and night and pollute the air in the area.
The speaker is arguing against the idea that _____
_____ .

DISCUSSION

SYNTHESIZING

7 Work in small groups. Use ideas from Listening 1 and Listening 2 to answer the following questions.

1 What are some of the similarities between hydroponics and nuclear energy? What are some of the differences?
2 Do you think nuclear power is a good energy solution? Why / Why not?
3 What do you think is the best form of energy? Why?

SPEAKING

CRITICAL THINKING

At the end of this unit, you are going to do the speaking task below.

> Take part in a debate about allowing a new wind farm near your town. You are a member of a town council. Some members of the council want a wind farm to be built. Argue for or against building a wind farm near your town.

Making counter-arguments

Use counter-arguments to help make your point stronger. To make an effective counter-argument, first show that you understand the opposing viewpoint.

Some people think that solar and wind energy are greener than nuclear energy.

Then, explain the weaknesses of the opposing viewpoint.

But I don't think that's accurate. Wind turbines are not exactly friendly for birds, not to mention that solar panels and wind turbines take up a lot of space.

1 Complete the table. Make notes about the opinions of the speakers in Listening 2. Use your notes from Exercise 4 on page 49 to help you.

UNDERSTAND

	for / against nuclear power	arguments	counter-arguments
Emma			
Jack			

2 Work with a partner. Compare your tables. Add or change any information as necessary. Tell your partner whether you agree more with Emma or Jack. Do you agree with your partner? Why / Why not?

 EVALUATE

3 Work in small groups. Think of some of the advantages and disadvantages of building a wind farm near your town, on a large, empty piece of land. Write your ideas in the table. Then, decide whether you are for or against the wind farm.

advantages of a wind farm	disadvantages of a wind farm

Overall, I am *for / against* building a wind farm near our town.

 APPLY

4 Write your best ideas from Exercise 3 in the *arguments* column. Remember, your arguments must relate to your opinion, so include advantages OR disadvantages – not both.

for / against wind farm	arguments	counter-arguments

5 Look at your ideas in Exercise 3 which support the opposite viewpoint. Think of what you will say in response to those arguments to make your argument stronger. Write your ideas in the *counter-arguments* column in the table in Exercise 4.

LINKING IDEAS WITH TRANSITION WORDS AND PHRASES

SKILLS

Speakers use transition words and phrases to link ideas. Different words and phrases are used for different purposes.

to explain a sequence of ideas	to compare and contrast ideas	to add another idea	to summarize ideas
first of all	and yet	and	all in all
first	though	also	to sum up
to begin with	but	on top of that	overall
second	on the other hand	in addition	in short
next	in comparison	plus	
finally		not to mention (that)	

There are numerous benefits of wind power. **First of all**, it is a clean source of energy.

Governments tell us that nuclear power is clean and safe **and yet** there have been a number of serious incidents around the world.

Burning fossil fuels causes serious pollution problems, **not to mention** the environmental damage caused by things like oil spills.

All in all, I think wind and solar power are the best ways to meet our country's energy needs.

1 Circle the correct word or phrase in the sentences. Think about the purpose of the words to help you choose the right answer.

1 In my opinion, nuclear energy is safe. *Also / Though*, it's cheap and clean.

2 Solar energy is an unlimited source of energy. *On the other hand / On top of that*, it's safe and environmentally friendly.

3 Wind turbines don't destroy the landscape. *And yet / Plus*, they can be dangerous for birds.

4 There are many reasons why we should build a solar power plant. *In addition / First of all*, solar energy is affordable and safe.

5 I think that nuclear power plants look ugly and destroy the landscape. *In addition / Finally*, they don't always provide jobs for local people.

PLUS

2 Read extracts from a discussion about building a new nuclear power plant near a city. Complete the extracts with words and phrases from the box.

> addition   ~~begin~~   comparison   first of all
> and yet   overall   second   the other hand

A: I would like to say that I completely disagree with the idea of building a nuclear power plant so close to the city. To (1)_____ **begin** _____ with, I understand that modern nuclear power plants are safer than they used to be and that the plant would be far from our homes. (2)_____ I worry about my children. If there is a nuclear disaster, our children will be exposed to radiation.

B: I have to agree with this. I worry about the nuclear waste. There are two big questions here. (3)_____ , how can we make sure that it doesn't leak into our water supply or soil? (4)_____ , where are we going to get rid of the nuclear waste? I don't think the government should go ahead with this project. Instead, we could build a solar power plant. It would be cleaner. So, (5)_____ , I think that solar energy would be the best option.

C: I don't think it's completely true that solar panels are better than nuclear energy. Solar power is very expensive to set up and then what? In (6)_____ , a nuclear power plant would be cheaper in the long term. And it would create more jobs.

D: I agree that our city needs more jobs. In (7)_____ , we need cheap, affordable energy. On the one hand, it's clear that a nuclear power plant will solve both these problems. On (8)_____ , I worry about the plant being so close to our homes. I suggest that we build it as far from the city as possible.

TALKING ABOUT ADVANTAGES AND DISADVANTAGES

3 Look at the extracts from a debate about solar energy. Do the words and phrases in bold refer to advantages or disadvantages? Write *A* (advantage) or *D* (disadvantage).

1 In my opinion, there are many **pros** of solar energy. _____
2 Personally, I think that solar energy **has a negative effect on** our wildlife. _____
3 **The good thing about** solar energy is that it's cheap. _____
4 The main **benefit** of solar energy is that it's environmentally friendly. _____
5 There are several **cons** of using solar energy. _____
6 The second **drawback** of solar energy is that solar farms are unattractive. _____

4 Complete the sentences with your own ideas.

1 The biggest drawback of nuclear energy is that …

_____.

2 There are many benefits of electric cars. For example, …

_____.

3 There are many pros and cons of using wind power. For instance, …

_____.

4 There are many disadvantages of using petrol. For example, …

_____.

GIVING COUNTER-ARGUMENTS

5 For each argument write a counter-argument. Use a word or phrase from the box and then add your ideas.

> yet   but (x2)   that's completely true

1 People often say that nuclear energy is dangerous, _but there
have been very few nuclear power accidents._

2 Some people say that solar power is the best kind of energy. I'm not sure _____

_____.

3 It may be true that fossil fuels have a negative effect on the environment. And _____

_____.

4 Electric cars are environmentally friendly, _____

_____.

6 Work with a partner. Look back at the sentences in Exercises 3, 4 and 5. Discuss which of the statements you agree with, and which you disagree with. Give reasons.

SPEAKING TASK

▶ Take part in a debate about allowing a new wind farm near your town. You are a member of a town council. Some members of the council want a wind farm to be built. Argue for or against building a wind farm near your town.

PREPARE

1 Look at the tables you created in Exercises 3–5 in the Critical thinking section. Review your notes with a partner who has the same opinion about the wind farm as you. Add any new information.

2 Refer to the Task checklist below as you prepare your arguments. You can use language like this:

In my opinion, there are many pros/cons ...
First of all, I think that ...
The main benefit/drawback is ...
A second benefit/drawback is ...
To sum up, ...

3 Prepare some notes about your counter-arguments. You can use language like this:

It may be true that ...
But ...
And yet ...

TASK CHECKLIST	✔
Use clear arguments and counter-arguments.	
Link ideas effectively with transition words and phrases.	
Explain advantages and disadvantages in a clear way.	
Use modals to express future possibility.	
Use negative prefixes correctly, where appropriate.	

PRACTISE

4 Work in a group of three with people who have the same viewpoint as you. Practise explaining why you are in favour of or against the wind farm.

5 Think about your arguments. Discuss ways to improve them.

DISCUSS

6 Work in a group of four. Your group should have two people with each viewpoint. Discuss your ideas and together decide whether the town would be better with a wind farm.

7 Present your group's decision to the class and explain your reasons.

OBJECTIVES REVIEW

1 Check your learning objectives for this unit. Write *3, 2* or *1* for each objective.

3 = very well   2 = well   1 = not so well

I can ...

watch and understand a video about offshore wind farms. _____

listen for explanations. _____

listen for counter-arguments. _____

make counter-arguments. _____

use modals to express future possibility. _____

link ideas with transition words and phrases. _____

talk about advantages and disadvantages. _____

give counter-arguments. _____

take part in a debate about allowing a new wind farm near my town. _____

2 Go to the *Unlock* Online Workbook for more practice with this unit's learning objectives.

 UNLOCK ONLINE

WORDLIST

affordable (adj)	environmental (adj) ⊙	provide (v) ⊙
alternative (adj) ⊙	limited (adj) ⊙	resource (n) ⊙
benefit (n) ⊙	long-term (adj) ⊙	risk (n) ⊙
crisis (n) ⊙	opponent (n) ⊙	solution (n) ⊙
disaster (n) ⊙	pollute (v)	system (n) ⊙

⊙ = high-frequency words in the Cambridge Academic Corpus

LEARNING OBJECTIVES

IN THIS UNIT YOU WILL ...

Watch and listen	watch and understand a video about the air travel revolution.
Listening skill	listen for rhetorical questions.
Critical thinking	evaluate problems and propose solutions.
Grammar	use comparative and superlative adjectives.
Speaking skills	give recommendations; expand on an idea.
Speaking task	give a presentation on a transport problem and suggest solutions to solve the problem.

TRANSPORT

UNL🔒CK YOUR KNOWLEDGE

Work with a partner. Discuss the questions.

1 What are some problems with modern forms of transport?
2 How has transport changed in the last 50 years?
3 What do you think is the future of transport? How will it be different in 50 years?

PLUS

PREPARING TO WATCH

1 Work with a partner. Discuss the questions.

1 Which two places in the world would you like to visit? How long would it take to fly to them? How much would it cost?

2 How did people travel between continents before there were aeroplanes?

2 Work with a partner. Look at the photos from the video and discuss the questions.

1 When you think about how far apart two places are, do you think of the distance in kilometres or in minutes or hours?

2 What city do you think the planes are flying over in the first two photos?

3 How has air travel changed the way that we think about our world?

> **GLOSSARY**
>
> **in no time** (idm) very quickly
>
> **revolutionize** (v) to change something completely so that it is much better than before
>
> **commercial plane** (n phr) a plane which carries passengers or goods; not a military or private plane
>
> **airspace** (n) the air or sky above a place

WHILE WATCHING

3 ▶ Complete the paragraph with the words in the box. Then, watch the video and check your answers.

> busiest   business   closer   commercial   larger   smaller

In the past 50 years, we've made the world [1]_____ . Cities and continents are [2]_____ than ever before. Many [3]_____ people travel great distances every week. Some [4]_____ planes are bigger than houses. The airspace above London is one of the [5]_____ in the world. The number of people travelling by plane grows [6]_____ every year.

4 ▶ Watch the video again. Circle the words which you hear.

1 Today we can travel from continent to continent *in time / in no time*.
2 South America and *Africa / Asia* are less than a day away from each other.
3 Military planes travel faster than the speed of *sound / light*.
4 Every day *350 / 3,500* flights take place overhead.
5 In *2015 / 2016*, about 3.7 billion people travelled by plane.
6 Right now, around the world, *over / under* a million people are travelling in the air.

DISCUSSION

5 Work in small groups. Take turns discussing the questions. Give reasons and examples for your answers.

1 Which do you think has changed the world more: the car or the aeroplane?
2 How would you describe the average airline customer in your country?
3 How do you think air travel has changed international business?

LISTENING

LISTENING 1

PRONUNCIATION FOR LISTENING

> **Word stress**
>
> Some words have the same form whether they are a noun or a verb.
>
> In recent years, there has been a significant **decrease** in the number of plane crashes. (*decrease* = noun)
> The number of plane crashes will **decrease** even more as planes become safer. (*decrease* = verb)
>
> However, the pronunciation may not be the same. In many two-syllable words, nouns are stressed on the first syllable and verbs on the second syllable.
> de̲crease (= noun)   decrea̲se (= verb)
>
> Note that not all words follow this pattern.
> contro̲l (= noun)   contro̲l (= verb)

1 🔊 3.1 Listen to the two sentences and answer the questions.

   1 There has been an **increase** in motorcycle accidents over the past five years.
   2 Airlines are always looking for new ways to **increase** the safety of their planes.

   a In which sentence is *increase* a verb? _____
   b In which sentence is *increase* a noun? _____
   c Where is the stress in each word? Circle the stressed syllable in each of the words.

2 🔊 3.2 Listen and circle the stressed syllable in the words in bold.

   1 There's a detailed **record** of each plane crash.
   2 A machine called a 'black box' **records** everything the pilot and co-pilot say during a flight.
   3 Some cities don't **permit** cycling on the pavement.
   4 I'm sorry, but you need an employee parking **permit** to park in this garage.
   5 The company **presents** an award for road safety to the safest city.
   6 He received a new car as a **present** from his parents.

3 Practise saying the sentences in Exercise 2.

PREPARING TO LISTEN

UNDERSTANDING
KEY VOCABULARY

4 You are going to listen to a radio interview with someone who worked for an airline. Before you listen, read the definitions. Complete the sentences with the correct form of the words in bold.

> **avoid** (v) to stay away from something or not allow yourself to do something
> **compare** (v) to look for the difference between two or more things
> **consist of** (phr v) to be made of something
> **crash** (n) an accident in which a vehicle hits something
> **cure** (n) something which will make an ill person healthy again
> **extreme** (adj) very severe or bad
> **safety** (n) the condition of not being in danger
> **scared** (adj) feeling frightened or worried

1 When there are _____ weather conditions, such as a big snowstorm or a hurricane, airports sometimes close.
2 Before you book a flight, be sure to _____ prices from different airlines to get the best deal.
3 There was a five-car _____ on the motorway this morning. Fortunately, everyone survived.
4 I try to _____ driving to work because the traffic is terrible. I usually take the underground instead.
5 There isn't a _____ for the common cold, but washing your hands often can help to protect you from colds.
6 The word *aerophobia* comes from the Greek and it _____ two parts: *aero*, which means 'flight' or 'air', and *phobia*, which means 'fear'.
7 If you're _____ of flying, you're not alone. About 25% of people have a fear of flying.
8 _____ is very important to airlines. They inspect their planes before every flight.

5 Work in small groups and discuss the questions.

1 Do you enjoy flying? Why / Why not?
2 Which of these forms of transport do you think is the most dangerous? Which do you think is the safest? Why?

a flying
b travelling by car

c travelling by motorcycle
d walking

WHILE LISTENING

6 🔊 3.3 Listen to the first part of a radio programme and circle the correct answer.

1 What is the main idea of the programme?
   a the history of aeroplanes
   b the fear of flying and how to reduce it
   c plane crash investigations
2 What did Mark use to be?
   a He was a flight attendant.
   b He was a psychologist.
   c He was a pilot.
3 What did Mark do to help himself?
   a He searched for advice on the internet.
   b He talked to his friends.
   c He studied air safety.
4 Can a fear of flying be cured?
   a Yes, but not always.
   b Yes, anyone can get rid of the fear of flying.
   c No, it can't.

7 🔊 3.4 Listen to the second part of the radio programme. Complete the notes using the words in the box.

| avoid | damaged | driving | engines | flying | normal | reduce | wings |

Steps you can take to (1)_____ the fear of flying:
- Learn how a plane works – helps you understand planes can fly without the (2)_____ because the (3)_____ push against the air + keep plane flying
- Turbulence is (4)_____ and can only cause an accident if plane is already (5)_____ or during a storm
- Learn where things are on a plane
- (6)_____ disaster movies
- Be realistic – remember (7)_____ is much safer than (8)_____

8 Work with a partner. Read the list of tips on how to deal with and control a fear of flying. How useful do you think each tip is? Discuss your ideas.

1 ☐ Learn how aeroplanes work.
2 ☐ Imagine you are on a bus or train.
3 ☐ Take something to help you sleep on the plane.
4 ☐ Learn the layout of the plane before takeoff.
5 ☐ Go to a psychologist.
6 ☐ Don't watch movies or TV shows about air disasters.

9 🔊 3.4 Listen to the second part of the radio programme again and tick the tips in Exercise 8 which Mark mentions.

LISTENING FOR DETAIL

POST-LISTENING

SKILLS

> ### Listening for rhetorical questions
>
> Rhetorical questions are an unusual type of question. Their purpose is to bring the listener's attention to a topic or an idea. The speaker does not expect an answer to the question.
>
> When you ask **regular questions**, you stop speaking and wait for an answer.
>
> When you ask **rhetorical questions**, you continue speaking.
>
> A: *So, is flying the safest way to travel?* (regular question, the speaker expects an answer)
>
> B: *Yes, I firmly believe that it is.*
>
> Presenter: *So, is flying the safest way to travel? The airlines will tell you it is, but not everyone is so confident.* (rhetorical question, the speaker does not expect an answer)

10 🔊 3.3 Listen to the first part of the radio programme again. Which questions are rhetorical questions? Which are regular questions? Tick your answers.

LISTENING FOR TEXT ORGANIZATION

	regular	rhetorical
1 Have you ever been afraid of flying?	☐	☐
2 Do you feel scared when you sit on a plane?	☐	☐
3 Are you stressed when there's turbulence?	☐	☐
4 Can you tell us more about your experience, Mark?	☐	☐
5 Did it make you afraid of flying?	☐	☐
6 What was I supposed to do?	☐	☐
7 Can it be cured?	☐	☐

DISCUSSION

11 Work in small groups. A phobia is an extreme fear of something. Look at the phobias and discuss the questions.

- *arachnophobia* – fear of spiders
- *trypanophobia* – fear of needles
- *ailurophobia* – fear of cats
- *aquaphobia* – fear of water
- *claustrophobia* – fear of being in a closed space
- *nomophobia* – fear of being outside of a mobile phone network
- *cynophobia* – fear of dogs
- *acrophobia* – fear of heights

1 Do you know anyone with a phobia? What phobia does the person have?
2 What do you think are the most common phobias?
3 Do you think it's possible to cure a phobia? If yes, how?

⊙ LANGUAGE DEVELOPMENT

TALKING ABOUT PROBLEMS AND SOLUTIONS

1 Read the sentences. Circle the correct definition for the words and phrases in bold.

1 I read stories of people who managed to **control** their fear of flying.
   a to remove something
   b to limit something
   c to understand something

2 For someone who has to travel for work, aerophobia is a **serious** problem.
   a important; bad
   b funny
   c unusual or different

3 Most turbulence is normal and won't cause any **trouble**, so you shouldn't be scared of it.
   a delays
   b fear
   c problems

4 The course had a strong **impact** on me. I actually became very scared of being on a plane.
   a effect
   b difference
   c stress

5 There are several ways to reduce your fear of flying. The first **method** is to learn more about how planes work.
   a a way of doing something
   b an idea about something
   c an answer to something

6 The engine is broken. The mechanics are trying to **figure out** how to fix it.
   a to research a problem
   b to think about a problem until you know the answer
   c to use maths to find the answer to a problem

7 How did it **influence** you? Did it make you afraid of flying?
   a to affect how someone acts or thinks
   b to make someone feel scared
   c to make someone think about a problem

PLUS

2 Work with a partner. Discuss the questions.

1 What problems does your city have with transport?
2 Think of a problem you have had in your life. How did you solve it?
3 Think of a challenge you might face in the future. What do you need to figure out to solve it?

COMPARATIVE AND SUPERLATIVE ADJECTIVES

Comparative adjectives say how two people, things or ideas are different. *Superlative adjectives* compare a person, thing or idea to all others.

Spelling of comparative and superlative adjectives

For one-syllable adjectives, add -er or -est. When the last letter of the word is -e, only add -r or -st.

fast → fast**er** → the fast**est**
large → larg**er** → the larg**est**

For one-syllable adjectives which end in one vowel and one consonant, double the consonant and add -er or -est. Do not double the consonant w.

big → big**ger** → the big**gest** (but low → low**er** → the low**est**)

For two-syllable adjectives ending in -y, remove the -y and add -ier or -iest.

scary → scar**ier** → scar**iest**

For almost all adjectives with two or more syllables, use *more / less* or *the most / the least* before the adjective.

serious → **more/less** serious → the **most/least** serious

Some adjectives are irregular in the comparative and superlative forms.

good → **better** → the **best**

subject	verb	comparative adjective	*than*	object
Taking a train		greener		driving.
Flying	is	scarier	than	taking a train.
Driving		more affordable		flying.

subject	verb	*the*	superlative adjective	object
Walking			greenest	
Flying	is	the	scariest	form of transport.
Taking a bus			most affordable	

We can use adverbials to modify comparative and superlative adjectives. Stress the adverbials when you speak.

This car is **a lot** nicer than mine.
Flying is **by far** the most expensive form of transport.

3 Complete the table with the comparative and superlative forms of the adjective.

Adjective	Comparative form	Superlative form
fast	faster than	the fastest
safe		
comfortable		
healthy		
dangerous		
thin		
slow		
relaxing		
noisy		

PLUS

4 3.5 Listen to the sentences. Circle the syllable in each phrase in bold which has the most stress.

1 The course was a **lot** more challenging than I expected.
2 We can see that **by far the most affordable** form of transport is walking.
3 The risks of driving a car are **considerably more significant than** those of flying.
4 For me, flying is **much more comfortable than** travelling by train.
5 Taking a train is **definitely more relaxing than** driving.
6 Using the underground is **a lot faster than** travelling by bus at rush hour.
7 Driving is **considerably more expensive** than walking.
8 Cycling is **absolutely the healthiest** form of transport.

5 Answer the questions.

1 Which sentences in Exercise 4 use the comparative form? _____
2 Which sentences use the superlative form? _____
3 Which words or phrases are used to modify the comparatives or superlatives? Underline them.
4 What is the meaning of the words or phrases you underlined?

_____

6 Complete the sentences with the correct form (comparative or superlative) of the adjectives in brackets.

1 The _____ route to my office is not always the fastest, because there is often a lot of traffic. (direct)

2 I'm always _____ in a car than in a plane. (calm)

3 Using mobile phones while driving is the _____ driving safety issue. (serious)

4 Driving your own car is the _____ way to travel. (comfortable)

5 If you are in a hurry, it is often _____ to cycle than to drive a car. (fast)

6 Buying a monthly pass for public transport is _____ than paying for every trip. (affordable)

7 In many countries the _____ tip for a taxi driver is 20% of the fare. (appropriate)

8 Many people are scared of flying, but flying is a lot _____ than driving. (safe)

7 Make a list of the types of transport in a city you know. Then, write sentences comparing the types of transport. Use comparative or superlative adjectives and adverbials to modify the adjectives.

1 <u>The underground is much faster than the bus.</u>

2 <u>Driving is definitely the most expensive type of transport.</u>

3 _____

4 _____

5 _____

6 _____

8 Work with a partner. Read your partner's sentences in Exercise 7. Do you agree or disagree with them? Why?

LISTENING 2

PREPARING TO LISTEN

1 You are going to listen to a presentation about cycling to work. Before you listen, read the sentences (1–8) below and write the words in bold next to the definitions (a–h).

1 Did you **injure** your knee when you fell off your bicycle?
2 Drivers should always have **respect** for pedestrians and stop for them.
3 I got a **fine** for driving through a red light. It was over £50.
4 Some teenagers **break the law** by driving without a licence.
5 We can **prevent** accidents by driving within the speed limit.
6 Many accidents happen when drivers **pass** other cars without checking their mirrors.
7 Many people drive cars to work because it's more **convenient** to sit comfortably in your own vehicle.
8 Our city has a lot of traffic problems. To **solve** some of them, we're encouraging people to cycle more and drive less.

a _____ (adj) easy to use or suiting your plans well
b _____ (v) to go past someone or something
c _____ (v) to hurt or cause physical harm
d _____ (n) polite behaviour towards someone
e _____ (v) to find a way to fix a problem
f _____ (n) money which has to be paid as a punishment for not obeying a law
g _____ (v) to stop something from happening
h _____ (v phr) to fail to obey the rules of a country, state or city

PLUS

2 Work with a partner and discuss the questions.

1 What are some of the reasons that people cycle in a big city?
2 What are some advantages of cycling to work?
3 What are some problems with cycling to work?

WHILE LISTENING

3 🔊 3.6 Listen to the first part of the presentation and answer the questions.

1 What is the goal of the Wheels to Work organization?

_____

2 What three main issues with cycling to work does the speaker mention?

a _____

b _____

c _____

4 🔊 3.6 Listen to the first part of the presentation again. Tick the problems the speaker mentions.

1 ☐ Most people don't have bicycles.
2 ☐ There's a lot of traffic.
3 ☐ There aren't any cycle lanes in the city.
4 ☐ The cycle lanes are often too narrow.
5 ☐ Cars sometimes drive in the cycle lanes.
6 ☐ There's nowhere to put your bicycle while you're working.
7 ☐ It's too cold.
8 ☐ There's nowhere to shower at work.
9 ☐ Some people live far away from work.
10 ☐ People don't want to cycle at night.

5 🔊 3.7 Listen to the second part of the presentation. What recommendations does the speaker make? What would be the results of the recommendations? Take notes.

recommendations	possible results
1	
2	
3	
4	
5	

POST-LISTENING

6 🔊 3.7 Listen to the second part of the presentation again. Tick the expressions which are used to introduce recommendations.

1 ☐ I'd suggest that …
2 ☐ I think it would be much better if …
3 ☐ I'd like to see …
4 ☐ I think it would be safer if …
5 ☐ We should …
6 ☐ I'd like it if …
7 ☐ (They) ought to …
8 ☐ In my opinion, we should …
9 ☐ The best thing would be if …

7 Work with a partner. What could be done to improve the transport system in your town or city? Take turns proposing ideas. Use some of the expressions in Exercise 6.

DISCUSSION

8 Work in small groups. Use ideas from Listening 1 and Listening 2 to answer the following questions.

1 Flying is much safer than cycling, yet most people have a greater fear of flying than of cycling. Why do you think this is?
2 Do you think the ideas from Listening 2 would work to encourage more cycling in your town or city? If not, what ideas would work? Why?

SPEAKING

CRITICAL THINKING

At the end of this unit, you are going to do the speaking task below.

Give a presentation on a transport problem and suggest solutions to solve the problem.

SKILLS

Evaluating problems and proposing solutions

When you think about a problem, you may be able to identify more than one possible solution. Try to decide which one is the best by predicting the probable results of each solution.

UNDERSTAND

1 Complete the table with the problems, proposed solutions and predicted results from Listening 2. Use information from your notes on page 72.

problems	proposed solutions	predicted results

2 Work with a partner. Compare your answers. Add any necessary information to your table.

3 Work with a partner. Think about the transport problems in your city or country. Write a list of the problems.

REMEMBER

4 Choose a transport problem. Write it in the *problems* column of the presentation planning table below. What are some possible solutions to the problem? Write them in the *proposed solutions* column.

APPLY

problems	proposed solutions	predicted results

5 What do you predict the results would be of each solution? Write your ideas in the *predicted results* column above. Which solution do you think is best? Circle it.

ANALYZE

6 Tell another pair about your preferred solution and why you think it is best. Do they agree?

GIVING RECOMMENDATIONS

SKILLS

Speakers use certain phrases to give recommendations, that is, ideas about what they think is the best thing to do. Here are some phrases you can use to give recommendations:

In my opinion, we should ...
We ought to ...
I'd like it if ...
I think it would be better if ...
The best thing would be ...
I (don't) think ...
I'd like to see ...
I'd suggest that ...
In my opinion, we should / We ought to do more to keep cyclists safe on the roads.
I'd like it if / I think it would be better if we had wider cycle lanes.
The best thing would be to have more places in the city to store bicycles.
I don't think the city should have more cycle lanes.
I'd like to see cycle racks on buses.
I'd suggest that we put cycle racks on buses.

1 🔊 3.8 Listen to a group discussion about the problem of eating while driving. Who do you agree with most? _____

2 Look at the extracts. Underline the phrases which introduce a recommendation or proposal.

  1 <u>I don't think</u> the government should do anything about it.
  2 I think it would be better if they closed drive-through restaurants.
  3 I think it would be much better if drivers weren't allowed to eat or drink while they drive.
  4 The best thing would be to have more cameras on the roads to record what drivers are doing.
  5 I'd suggest that the police give the drivers points on their licence.

EXPANDING ON AN IDEA

When speakers propose an idea or make a recommendation, they often state the idea first and then give more details about it. Details can include reasons and examples from personal experience.

Idea: *I think it would be better if they closed drive-through restaurants.*

Reason: *This is because they only encourage drivers to buy food and eat it while they drive.*

Example from personal experience: *Last week, I bought some coffee and something to eat on the way to work …*

3 The speakers in the group discussion expand on their ideas. Match the details (a–d) to the ideas in Exercise 2 (1–5). There is one extra idea.

  a From my own experience, I can tell you that it can be very dangerous. __3__

  b Personally, I eat fast food in my car a few times a week and I've never had an accident. _____

  c The reason for this is the police can check the videos to see who's eating, who's texting and so on. _____

  d This is because they only encourage drivers to buy food and eat it while they drive. _____

4 Work with a partner. What is your opinion of eating while driving? Discuss your opinion. Give recommendations and examples from personal experience or knowledge. Do you agree with each other?

> Give a presentation on a transport problem and suggest solutions to solve the problem.

PREPARE

1 Look at the table you created in Exercises 4 and 5 in the Critical thinking section. Review your notes and add any new information.

2 Refer to the Task checklist below as you prepare your presentation. You can use language like this:

I'd suggest ...   The best thing would be ...
I think it would be better if ...   I'd like to see ...
In my opinion, we should ...

3 For each proposed solution, make notes about how you will expand on your idea with reasons and examples from personal experience or knowledge. You can use language like this:

The reason for this is ...
This is because ...
From my own experience ...
Personally, ...

TASK CHECKLIST	✔
Compare different options.	
Propose ideas clearly.	
Expand on ideas by giving reasons.	
Talk about personal experiences clearly.	

PRACTISE

4 Work in small groups. Take turns practising your presentations. Take notes during the discussion. Use your notes to give feedback to each other to improve your presentations.

PRESENT

5 Take turns giving your presentation to the class.

OBJECTIVES REVIEW

1 Check your learning objectives for this unit. Write *3*, *2* or *1* for each objective.

3 = very well   2 = well   1 = not so well

I can ...

watch and understand a video about the air travel revolution. _____

listen for rhetorical questions. _____

evaluate problems and propose solutions. _____

use comparative and superlative adjectives. _____

give recommendations. _____

expand on an idea. _____

give a presentation on a transport problem and suggest solutions to solve the problem. _____

2 Go to the *Unlock* Online Workbook for more practice with this unit's learning objectives.

 UNLOCK ONLINE

WORDLIST		
avoid (v) 𝇈	extreme (adj) 𝇈	prevent (v) 𝇈
break the law (v phr)	figure out (phr v)	respect (n) 𝇈
compare (v) 𝇈	fine (n) 𝇈	safety (n) 𝇈
consist of (phr v)	impact (n) 𝇈	scared (adj)
control (v) 𝇈	influence (v) 𝇈	serious (adj) 𝇈
convenient (adj) 𝇈	injure (v)	solve (v) 𝇈
crash (n)	method (n) 𝇈	trouble (n) 𝇈
cure (n) 𝇈	pass (v) 𝇈	

𝇈 = high-frequency words in the Cambridge Academic Corpus

IN THIS UNIT YOU WILL ...

Watch and listen	watch and understand a video about the Chinese tradition of moon cakes.
Listening skills	identify cause and effect; listen for opinion.
Critical thinking	create a convincing argument.
Grammar	use dependent prepositions.
Speaking skills	be polite in a discussion; use adverbs for emphasis; use phrases with *that*.
Speaking task	take part in a discussion about whether special occasions have become too commercial.

UNLOCK YOUR KNOWLEDGE

Work in small groups. Discuss the questions.

1 Look at the photo. What country do you think it is from? What is the tradition?

2 Do you have any similar traditions in your country?

3 Do you follow all of your country's traditional customs? Why / Why not?

PLUS

WATCH AND LISTEN

PREPARING TO WATCH

ACTIVATING YOUR
KNOWLEDGE

1 Work with a partner. Discuss the questions.

1 What is a harvest? Is there a harvest festival in your country? If so, when is it and what happens?

2 Are there any events or traditions in your country which are connected to the moon? If so, what are they?

3 At what festivals in your country do people eat particular foods? What are these foods? Do you know why people eat them?

PREDICTING
CONTENT USING
VISUALS

2 You are going to watch a video about food which people eat at a harvest festival. Before you watch, look at the pictures. Discuss the questions with your partner.

1 Look at picture 1. What part or parts of the world do you think this festival takes place in?

2 Look at picture 2. What do you see the chef mixing in the picture?

3 Look at picture 3. What do you think the chef will do in the video?

4 Look at picture 4 and read the glossary. What can you see in this picture?

GLOSSARY

filling (n) food that is put inside things, such as cakes, sandwiches, etc.

paste (n) a soft food which can be used to put on bread, fill cakes, etc.

layer (n) a flat, thin piece of something which covers something else

pastry (n) a food made from flour, butter or oil, and water, cooked and used to cover or hold other food

mould (n) an object that is used to make something in a particular shape

decoration (n) attractive patterns or objects put on something else to make it look nice

WHILE WATCHING

3 ▶ Watch the video and check your ideas in Exercise 2. Then, answer the questions.

1 How do people celebrate the Mid-Autumn Festival?

_____

2 What is the traditional food of the festival? Why are they given that name?

_____

3 Is the traditional food easy to make? Why / Why not?

_____

4 ▶ Put the stages in the recipe in order (1–8). Watch again and check.

_____ a Add the other filling ingredients, such as sweet beans.

_____ b Leave for at least one day before serving.

_____ c Cover balls of filling with a layer of pastry.

_____ d Bake in the oven until golden brown.

___1___ e Mix butter and sugar together well.

_____ f Use a mould to shape and decorate each cake.

_____ g Mix the filling until it is smooth and thick.

_____ h Use a brush to cover the top with egg.

5 ▶ Watch again. Correct the mistakes in each sentence.

1 The Mid-Autumn Festival is only celebrated in China.
2 Chinese people like to make moon cakes at home.
3 Moon cakes are traditionally filled with black beans and sweet eggs.
4 The decorations on the top of moon cakes are always Chinese letters.
5 After the moon cakes are made, they are left for the pastry to become hard.

DISCUSSION

6 Work in small groups. Discuss the questions.

1 Which festival foods are usually made at home in your country? Who prepares these in your family? How long does it take? What are the main ingredients?
2 Which foods that people eat at festivals are usually bought from shops? Why? Do you think people buy more festival foods from shops than they used to? Why? / Why not?
3 Do you ever give food as a gift? When? What? Do you usually make it at home or buy it from shops? Why?

LISTENING

LISTENING 1

PREPARING TO LISTEN

UNDERSTANDING
KEY VOCABULARY

1 You are going to listen to a podcast about customs in the modern world. Before you listen, circle the correct definitions for the words in bold.

1 My neighbourhood is very **multicultural**. People of many cultures and religions live here.
   a busy and crowded due to a lack of space for housing
   b including people who have many different customs and beliefs

2 The tradition of letter writing has almost **died out**. These days, everyone communicates by social media, texting or email.
   a to become rare and then disappear
   b to change into something else

3 Min-Soo **interacts** with a lot of people all day at work, so when he gets home, he likes to relax and spend some time alone.
   a to avoid doing things with other people
   b to communicate and do things with someone or something

4 Tomorrow is my 10th work **anniversary**. I can't believe I've had this job for ten years!
   a a job that you have enjoyed working in for a long time
   b the day on which an important event happened in a previous year

5 In the United States, most families have a **celebration** at Thanksgiving. They get together with family and friends to enjoy a big meal.
   a a trip to another country or to visit family
   b doing something to mark a special day or event

6 A few **generations** ago, people listened to the radio at night instead of watching TV or going online.
   a all the people of about the same age within a society or a family
   b a period of time lasting for several months

7 Anna has had an active **political** career. She was on the city council for several years and then she was elected to the national government.
   a relating to a person's job
   b relating to the government

8 **Social** anthropologists study the ways in which people live in groups around the world.
   a relating to a large group of people who live together in an organized way
   b relating to countries and their systems of government

2 Work with a partner. Discuss the questions.

 1 What does *tradition* mean? What are the most important customs and traditions in your country or your family? Why are they important?

 2 What are some ways that technology has changed people's daily lives in the past 25 years? Do you think these changes are positive or negative? Would your parents or grandparents agree with you?

USING YOUR KNOWLEDGE

WHILE LISTENING

3 🔊 4.1 Listen to an advertisement for a podcast. Answer the questions.

 1 Who is Dr Kevin Lee?

 _____

 2 What is the main topic of discussion on the podcast?

 _____

LISTENING FOR MAIN IDEAS

4 🔊 4.2 Listen to the podcast. Which picture shows a tradition the speaker doesn't mention? _____

5 🔊 4.2 Listen to the podcast again. Write notes in the table.

Effects of modern technology on traditions

	old tradition	new tradition
sending cards or messages	people sent cards	people send messages through social networking or by text or email
preparing holiday food		
recipes		
where people eat holiday meals		

POST-LISTENING

SKILLS

Identifying cause and effect

During a lecture or presentation, a speaker sometimes talks about causes and effects. To identify causes, listen for phrases like: *Due to ...* , *The reason for this is ...* , *because ...* , etc.

Due to modern kitchens, (cause) people don't have to spend much time cooking any more. (effect)

People don't have to spend much time cooking any more. (effect) **The reason for this is** (that) we have modern kitchens. (cause)

To identify **effects**, listen for phrases like *That's why ...* , *This means ...* , etc.

As a child, I lived in Japan, Thailand and Egypt. (cause) **That's why** I decided to study Anthropology. (effect)

You can find any recipe you want on the internet. (cause) **This means that** many people don't need cookbooks any more. (effect)

6 🔊 4.3 Listen and complete the extracts from the podcast.

1 Anthropology, in a general sense, is the study of humanity. I know that's not very exact. _____ we have many types of Anthropology, like Linguistic anthropology and Social anthropology.

2 Some traditions die out _____ our way of life changes.

3 Now, _____ developments in technology, people spend more time interacting with other people over the internet.

4 But now we don't have to work so hard. _____ we have modern kitchens and supermarket food.

5 In the United States, at Thanksgiving, which is one of the biggest celebrations, many families go to restaurants _____ they don't want to spend their holiday working in the kitchen.

7 Work with a partner. Underline the cause and circle the effect in each sentence in Exercise 6.

8 Circle the best word or phrase to complete each sentence.

1 *Because / This means that* people spend more time online, our social lives have changed.

2 Both of my parents work full-time. *That's why / The reason for this is* they don't have much time to cook at home.

3 We have developed new technology. *Due to / This means that* our habits have changed.

4 People don't buy many CDs any more *because / that's why* you can buy digital music.

5 *The reason for this is / Because of* social networking sites, people communicate more over the internet.

PRONUNCIATION FOR LISTENING

Connected speech: /t/ and /d/ at the end of words

When people speak quickly and naturally, the gaps between words are often not easy to hear and people don't always pronounce all the letters in a word. For example, they don't always pronounce the /t/ or /d/ sounds at the end of words if they are followed directly by a consonant sound.

Listen to this sentence. The letters highlighted in green are not pronounced clearly. The letter highlighted in yellow is pronounced clearly.

🔊 4.4 I study different cultures around the world and how social and political changes affect these cultures.

9 🔊 4.5 Listen to extracts from the podcast. Circle the /t/ and /d/ sounds which you can hear clearly in the bold words. In one sentence you don't need to circle any sounds.

1 My book is **about** the **effect** of modern technology on traditions **around** the world.
2 People **spent** a **lot** of time **and effort** preparing special meals.
3 Growing up in **different** cultures helps you realize **that** customs and traditions are often local.
4 We still **spend** time interacting with other people, **but** it's **not** always face-to-face.
5 In the **past**, people **sent** each other cards to celebrate **important** events, like an anniversary or a new baby.
6 Traditions **don't** always die out – **but** customs and traditions do change **and adapt** to the modern world.

DISCUSSION

10 Work in small groups. Discuss the questions.

1 What traditions in your country have changed in the last 20 years? Why have they changed?
2 Are the traditions or customs in your country similar to those in any other country you know?
3 Are there any traditions or customs in other countries which you would like to have in your own country?

SUFFIXES

A suffix is a group of letters which goes at the end of a word to make a new word. Learning the meaning of suffixes is a quick way to expand your vocabulary. Look at how some common suffixes change the meaning of a word.

word	suffix	new word	part of speech	meaning of suffix
tradition	-al	traditional	adjective	relating to
end	-less	endless	adjective	without
accept	-able*	acceptable	adjective	can
modern	-ize	modernize	verb	cause/become
strength	-en	strengthen	verb	changes a noun to a verb
develop	-ment	development	noun	action, result
prevent	-ion	prevention	noun	action, process
help	-ful	helpful	adjective	full of

* If a word ends in a consonant + *y*, change the *y* to *i* and add *able*: rely → reliable

1 Look at the suffixes at the end of the words in the box. Which part of speech is each word? Write the words in the correct column in the table.

agreement   celebration   communication   connection   digital
digitize   excitement   frighten   hopeful   organize   political
professional   recognize   specialize   successful   unbelievable
unforgettable   useless   weaken

adjective	verb	noun

2 Work with a partner. Can you think of more words that end in suffixes, as in the language box? Write them in the correct column in the table above. Use a dictionary to help you.

3 Correct the mistakes in bold using the word forms in brackets.

1 Chinese New Year is a great **celebrate**. (noun)

_____

2 I got 60% in my exam. That's **accept** but not great. (adjective)

_____

3 I'm in **agree** with you. Your argument really makes sense. (noun)

_____

4 The **politics** situation in this country is very stable. (adjective)

_____

5 Public speaking **frights** many people. It's one of the most common fears. (verb)

_____

6 I want to **special** in foreign languages. (verb)

_____

4 Complete the sentences with the correct form of the words in brackets.

1 A lot of people think that it's bad for teenagers to spend so much time on social networking sites, but I think it's _____ (harm). It's just fun!

2 You can find a lot of good, _____ (use) information on the internet. But to be honest, a lot of it is not _____ (rely). You need to be _____ (care) about your sources.

3 It's _____ (enjoy) to celebrate national holidays.

4 Some people might think you're not _____ (thought) if you don't remember their anniversary.

5 Work with a partner. Discuss the sentences in Exercise 4. Do you agree or disagree with each sentence? Why?

DEPENDENT PREPOSITIONS

Many verbs and adjectives are followed by specific prepositions. These are called *dependent prepositions*. It is important to remember these prepositions when you learn a new word. For example, the verb *adapt* is followed by the dependent preposition *to*.

Customs and traditions do change and **adapt to** the modern world.

Common verb + preposition combinations

belong to	listen to	talk to
laugh at	talk about	worry about

Common adjective + preposition combinations

bad for	full of	surprised by
excited about	responsible for	wrong with

You can sometimes put other words, such as adverbs, between a verb and a preposition.

We talked **excitedly** about our favourite moments from the festival.

GRAMMAR

6 Circle the correct prepositions. Use a dictionary to help you.

1 Do you adapt quickly *for / to* new situations?
2 Do you like listening *for / to* traditional music?
3 Are you excited *about / with* any events this year?
4 Do you think there is anything wrong *of / with* technology?
5 Do you worry *about / to* spending too much time online?
6 Do you belong *of / to* any clubs?
7 What is your favourite topic to talk *of / about*?
8 What did you laugh *at / of* recently?

PLUS

7 Work with a partner. Ask and answer the questions in Exercise 6. Give more information about your answer.

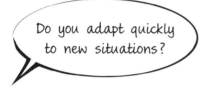

Do you adapt quickly to new situations?

No, I don't think so. It usually takes me some time to get used to new situations.

8 Complete the sentences with a preposition from the box. Use a dictionary to help you.

| about   by   for (x2)   in   to |

1 When did you first become interested _____ Anthropology?
2 Due _____ developments in technology, people communicate less face-to-face.
3 There are people who complain _____ the changes which technology has brought to our lives.
4 Looking at a screen for too long can be bad _____ your eyes.
5 I was surprised _____ the differences between people of different cultures.
6 My grandmother was responsible _____ making huge meals for our family celebrations.

PREPARING TO LISTEN

UNDERSTANDING
KEY VOCABULARY

1 You are going to listen to a discussion about gift giving. Before you listen, read the definitions. Complete the sentences with the correct form of the words in bold.

> **behaviour** (n) a particular way of acting
> **commercial** (adj) relating to buying and selling things
> **event** (n) anything which happens, especially something important or unusual
> **graduate** (v) to complete university or college successfully
> **obligation** (n) something which you have to do
> **occasion** (n) a special event or ceremony
> **personal** (adj) relating to an individual person and not anyone else
> **thoughtful** (adj) showing care and consideration in how you treat other people

1 Did you really want to go to that dinner or was it a(n) _____ ?
2 After I _____ from college, I'm going to have a big celebration.
3 To make the card more _____ , be sure to write a nice note inside.
4 To reward good _____ , Ms Martinez lets her students have extra time outside.
5 Thank you for the flowers for our anniversary. That was really

_____ .

6 Becca likes to wear casual clothes. She only gets dressed up on special

_____ .

7 Our company is having a special _____ to celebrate its best salespeople.
8 Holidays have become too _____ . People spend too much on gifts.

2 Work in small groups. Discuss the questions.

USING YOUR
KNOWLEDGE

1 On what occasions do people in your country usually give gifts? Who do they give gifts to?
2 Do you enjoy shopping for and giving gifts? Why / Why not?

WHILE LISTENING

3 🔊 4.6 Listen to the first part of the discussion. Circle the topic which the students are going to discuss.

a Is shopping fun?

b Are holidays too commercial?

c How do people celebrate Mother's Day?

4 🔊 4.7 Listen to the rest of the discussion. Do the speakers mention any of your ideas from Exercise 2, Question 1? Which ones?

_____

_____

LISTENING FOR MAIN IDEAS

5 🔊 4.8 Listen to the discussion again and take notes about the speakers' *yes* and *no* arguments. Write the reasons people give for their opinion.

Have special occasions become too commercial?

TAKING NOTES ON DETAIL

yes	no

6 Work with a partner. Compare your answers from the table above. Add information to your own table as necessary.

POST-LISTENING

SKILLS

Listening for opinion

When you listen, it is important to understand a speaker's opinion – that is, what the speaker thinks about a topic. To identify opinion, listen for phrases and expressions like these:

signposting an opinion	agreeing	disagreeing
It seems to me ...	I agree.	I'm not convinced.
What about ... ?	Yes, that's true.	I disagree.
Why not ... ?	That's right.	It's not true.
Personally, I ...	It's true.	I'm against ...
I think that ...	I couldn't agree more.	I don't agree.

7 🔊 4.9 Listen and complete the opinion phrases.

1 I ___couldn't agree___ more.

2 How did this whole gift giving for every holiday tradition get started, anyway? It _____ silly to me.

3 I _____ . I get tired of shopping for gifts.

4 I _____ . I like giving gifts.

5 But I'm _____ because then you have to spend money ... money which could be spent on more important things.

6 Instead, _____ write letters of advice for the future? That would be more special.

7 Sorry, I _____ . I doubt that graduates would be happy if we changed that custom!

DISCUSSION

SYNTHESIZING

8 Work in small groups. Use ideas from Listening 1 and Listening 2 to answer the following questions.

1 Do you think technology has changed gift-giving traditions? If so, how? Are these changes positive or negative?

2 What are your culture's customs for celebrating graduations? What is your opinion of these customs? Can you think of better ways to celebrate graduations?

PLUS

SPEAKING

CRITICAL THINKING

At the end of this unit, you are going to do the speaking task below.

> Take part in a discussion about whether special occasions have become too commercial.

Creating a convincing argument

A *convincing* argument is one that makes people believe it is right or true. The best way to make an argument convincing is to provide clear, persuasive reasons to support your point. To check if an argument is convincing, try telling a friend or classmate. Are they convinced? If not, what could you say to be more convincing?

1 Work with a partner. Look at your notes in the table in Listening 2. Write the arguments in the chart. Then, write ✓ (I agree) or ✗ (I disagree) next to each argument. Do you agree or disagree with your partner?

ANALYZE

	argument	✓ / ✗
Special occasions have become too commercial.		
Special occasions have not become too commercial.		

2 Work in small groups. Think of some more ideas for each side of the argument. Think about the holidays in your culture. Do you give gifts? Are those gifts meaningful? Are there any other events or occasions where people give gifts? Do you think giving these gifts is a good idea? Why / Why not?

REMEMBER

3 Write all of the ideas your group discussed in the table.

	arguments for the statement
Special occasions have become too commercial.	
Special occasions have not become too commercial.	

 **EVALUATE**

4 Look at the arguments in the two tables. Which side of the debate do you agree with? List the three main reasons for your opinion. Then, tell your group.

Reason 1: _____

_____

Reason 2: _____

_____

Reason 3: _____

_____

PREPARATION FOR SPEAKING

BEING POLITE IN A DISCUSSION

SKILLS

To have a good discussion, it is important to say when you agree and disagree with people. When you disagree, show that you understand and respect the other person's opinion.
You may be right, but …
I see your point, but …

You should also take turns and ask other people's opinions. You can do this by asking questions.
What do you think?
What's your opinion?

If you want to interrupt someone because you have a point to make, you can do it politely.
I'm sorry to interrupt, but …
Excuse me for interrupting, but …
Excuse me, can I say something?

1 Look at this discussion. Circle the best options.

A: I think holidays are too commercial. What do you think?

B: [1]*I'm sorry to interrupt / I see your point*, but I think people really enjoy giving and receiving gifts. It's a way to show you care about people.

A: [2]*I agree / You may be right, but* there are better ways to show you care. It can be more thoughtful to spend time with people than to give them gifts.

B: [3]*I understand, but / You misunderstood my point* can't you do both? I mean, there's no reason that you have to choose –

A: [4]*I see your point / I'm sorry to interrupt, but* I actually do feel like it's a choice. Sometimes I'm so busy doing holiday shopping that I don't have enough time to spend with my friends and family.

B: I'm sorry, but [5]*I disagree / I understand*. I think if you plan ahead and maybe shop online, shopping doesn't have to take a lot of time. You can give people nice gifts and also spend time with them.

2 Work with a partner. Follow the instructions.

Student A	Student B
• You think that it's good to relax on holidays. On special days, people should go out to dinner rather than cook. Cooking involves a lot of work and no one should have to work on holidays.	• Listen to Student A.
	• Say you understand, but traditions are important. People have always made traditional food on special days and they should continue to do that. Cooking is a way to show your family that you care about them.
• Listen to Student B.	
• Tell Student B your opinion.	• Tell Student A your opinion.

USING ADVERBS FOR EMPHASIS

We can use adverbs to make a point stronger.

I **strongly** believe that people spend too much money on gifts. (= I believe very much)

I **really** think that ...

You can use these adverbs when you are sure that you agree or disagree.

I **totally** agree. (= I agree 100%.)

Yes, that's **completely** true.

That's **definitely** right.

I'm **really not** convinced. (= I have very big doubts about your point.)

It's **absolutely not** true.

3 Look at the sentences. Circle the sentences that you agree with and change the sentences you disagree with. Add adverbs if you have a strong opinion.

1 It's true that people don't have time to cook any more.

_____

2 I'm against spending a lot of money during holidays or celebrations.

_____

3 I agree that modern technology has changed the way we interact with each other.

_____

4 It's true that travelling to other countries helps us understand other cultures and their traditions.

_____

5 I agree that tourists bring bad habits to our country.

_____

6 I don't believe that learning English affects local customs and traditions.

_____

4 Work with a partner. Compare your ideas from Exercise 3. Say if you agree or disagree with your partner.

PRONUNCIATION FOR SPEAKING

SKILLS

Stress patterns in phrases for agreeing and disagreeing

Speakers often stress adverbs for emphasis when they agree or disagree.

🔊 4.10 I **completely** agree that holidays have become too commercial.
I **absolutely** disagree that we should stop giving gifts on Mother's Day.
I **really** think that we should give fewer gifts.

5 Work with a partner. Underline the adverbs in the sentences. Then, practise saying the sentences. Remember to stress the adverbs.

1 I strongly believe that we should spend less time using social media.
2 I'm absolutely convinced that buying expensive cars is a waste of money.
3 I really think that we can learn a lot from older people.
4 I completely disagree with that argument.

PHRASES WITH *THAT*

> Phrases with *that* can be used to introduce an opinion or an idea.
>
> I think **that** ... ,   I believe **that** ...
>
> Many people believe **that** ...   I doubt **that** ...

6 Write *P* next to the sentences in which the speaker introduces a personal opinion. Write *O* next to the sentences in which the speaker refers to information from other people.

1 **I think that** it shows that you were thinking of someone. _____
2 **I've heard that** when people receive more than a few gifts, they usually can't even remember who gave them which gift. _____
3 **I believe that** we should learn about customs and traditions from different places. _____
4 **Many people say that** travel improves the mind. _____
5 **I disagree that** the internet has destroyed local customs and traditions. _____
6 **Everyone knows that** people usually buy gifts because it's an obligation, not because they really want to. _____
7 **I doubt that** graduates would be happy if we changed that custom! _____
8 **It's a well-known fact that** the internet has made it easier to communicate. _____

7 Complete the phrases with your own ideas.

1 I disagree that _____ .
2 I strongly believe that _____ .
3 It's a well-known fact that _____ .
4 Everyone knows that _____ .
5 I've heard that _____ .
6 I doubt that _____ .

8 Work with a partner. Discuss your ideas from Exercise 7.

SPEAKING TASK

▶ Take part in a discussion about whether special occasions have become too commercial.

PREPARE

1 Look at the table you created in Exercises 3 and 4 in the Critical thinking section. Review your notes and add any new information.

2 Work in small groups with students who have the same opinion as you. Look at the main points you want to make in the discussion and plan what language you will use to make these points. Make notes. You can use language like this:

It seems to me …

I think that …

What about … ?

I've heard that …

Why not … ?

It's a well-known fact that …

Personally, I …

3 Make a list of arguments to support the opposite opinion. Then, make notes about how you will respond to each argument. You can use language like this:

I see your point, but …

You may be right, but …

4 Refer to the Task checklist below as you prepare for your discussion.

TASK CHECKLIST	✔
Use adverbs for emphasis.	
Use phrases with *that* appropriately.	
Use suffixes and verbs and adjectives + prepositions appropriately.	
Interrupt, agree and disagree appropriately.	
Show respect for other people's opinions.	

PRACTISE

5 Work in groups of four. Two people should agree with one side of the argument and two with the opposite side. Practise having your discussion. Take notes on the other students' performance during the practice and feed back to them on how they could improve their points.

DISCUSS

6 Work with a different group. Discuss the topic with students who agree with you and who disagree with you.

OBJECTIVES REVIEW

1 Check your learning objectives for this unit. Write *3, 2* or *1* for each objective.

3 = very well   2 = well   1 = not so well

I can ...

watch and understand a video about the Chinese tradition
of moon cakes. _____

identify cause and effect. _____

listen for opinion. _____

create a convincing argument. _____

use dependent prepositions. _____

be polite in a discussion. _____

use adverbs for emphasis. _____

use phrases with *that*. _____

take part in a discussion about whether special occasions have
become too commercial. _____

2 Go to the *Unlock* Online Workbook for more practice with this unit's
learning objectives.

WORDLIST

acceptable (adj) ⦿	event (n) ⦿	occasion (n) ⦿
agreement (n) ⦿	frighten (v)	personal (adj) ⦿
anniversary (n)	generation (n) ⦿	political (adj) ⦿
behaviour (n) ⦿	graduate (v) ⦿	social (adj) ⦿
celebration (n)	interact (v)	specialize (v)
commercial (adj) ⦿	multicultural (adj)	thoughtful (adj)
die out (phr v)	obligation (n) ⦿	

⦿ = high-frequency words in the Cambridge Academic Corpus

HEALTH AND FITNESS

UNL⌀CK YOUR KNOWLEDGE

Work with a partner. Discuss the questions.

1 What are the people in the photo doing? Why do you think they're doing it?

2 What advice would you give to someone who wants to live to be 100 years old? What should the person do or not do?

3 Do you think it is easier or harder to stay healthy now than it was 100 years ago? Why?

PLUS

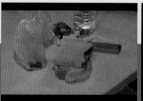

ACTIVATING YOUR KNOWLEDGE

PREPARING TO WATCH

1 Complete the questionnaire about health in your country.

Healthy living in _____

1 *Most / Some / A small number of* adults eat too much unhealthy food.

2 *Most / Some / A small number of* adults don't get enough exercise.

3 *Most / Some / A small number* of children eat too much unhealthy food.

4 *Most / Some / A small number* of adults don't get enough exercise.

---

2 Work with a partner. Explain your answers to the questionnaire. What do the results mean for your country?

PREDICTING CONTENT USING VISUALS

3 You are going to watch a video about healthy lifestyles in the UK. Look at the pictures and read the glossary. Tick the ideas you think you will hear in the video.

1 ☐ More people around the world are fat than in the past.
2 ☐ Unhealthy habits begin in childhood.
3 ☐ Children usually do more exercise than adults.
4 ☐ School lunches are healthier than lunches packed by their parents.
5 ☐ Most parents in the UK give their children unhealthy packed lunches.
6 ☐ Children can eat anything they want if they do a lot of exercise.

GLOSSARY

obese (adj) fat in a way that is dangerous for health

overweight (adj) being heavier than you want or than is good for you

PE (n, abbr) classes at school in which children do exercise and learn to play sport

on a mission (phr) trying to do something you think is important, but that is very difficult

packed lunch (n) a meal put in a bag or box, that you take with you to be eaten later, for example at school or work

protein (n) something found in food, such as meat, cheese, fish or eggs, that the body needs to grow and be strong

WHILE WATCHING

4 ▶ Watch the video and check your ideas in Exercise 3.

5 ▶ Watch again. Complete the missing numbers in the student's notes.

Obesity and childhood

The World • Three times more obese people than in (1)_____

• (2)_____ of children overweight or obese

The UK • (3)_____ children obese

• (4)_____ of packed lunches as healthy as
school lunches

• (5)_____ packed lunches include salad /
vegetables

• (6)_____ packed lunches include salty snacks

---

6 ▶ Watch again. Complete the sentences.

1 Most people live in countries where more people die from _____
_____ .

2 Laurence Clark wants to help children to _____
_____ .

3 In the study, all the healthy lunches included _____
_____ .

4 Most parents include unhealthy foods, such as _____
_____ .

5 The advice for parents is to _____
_____ .

DISCUSSION

7 Work in small groups. Discuss the questions.

1 How similar or different were your PE lessons at school to the ones
shown in the video?

2 What is in a typical packed lunch in your country? Do you think it is
healthy or unhealthy? Why?

LISTENING

LISTENING 1

PREPARING TO LISTEN

1 You are going to listen to a podcast about why some people live a long life. Before you listen, read the sentences (1–6) below and write the correct form of the words in bold next to the definitions (a–f).

1 My grandmother is very healthy. She's never had a serious **illness**.
2 Research **proves** that exercising can improve your health.
3 I have a **habit** of eating chocolate in the evenings. I eat it almost every night!
4 He has an **unhealthy** lifestyle. He never exercises and hardly ever eats fruit and vegetables.
5 Exercise is important to me, so I **work out** at the gym three mornings a week.
6 I'm a few pounds **overweight**. I should probably go on a diet.

a _____ (adj) not good for your health; not strong and well
b _____ (phr v) to exercise in order to make your body stronger
c _____ (v) to show that something is true
d _____ (n) a disease of the body or mind
e _____ (adj) being heavier than you want or than is good for you
f _____ (n) something which you do regularly

2 Work in a group and discuss the photos.

1 What are the differences between the lifestyles of the people in the photos?
2 How do you think different lifestyles can affect our health?
3 Do you think that the genes we receive from our parents can affect our health? How?

WHILE LISTENING

3 🔊 5.1 Listen to an introduction to a podcast and answer the questions.

1 Do people who live to be 100 years old always have a healthy lifestyle?

_____

2 What does the speaker say is more important than lifestyle for having a long and healthy life?

_____

4 🔊 5.2 Listen to the podcast and complete the notes.

Speaker A
I think (1)_____
I think that (2)_____
I'd much rather have pizza than go to the gym.
Speaker B
It's ridiculous to (3)_____
I'm sure that (4)_____
Speaker C
I prefer to (5)_____
I also think that you won't know you have the right genes until you get sick.
I'd say that (6)_____
There's no doubt that (7)_____
Speaker D
I'm sure that children won't have a long, healthy life if they eat junk food.
I prefer to (8)_____

PRONUNCIATION FOR LISTENING

SKILLS

Attitude and emotion

To understand a speaker's message, it is necessary to understand their attitude –
what they are thinking or feeling. This is especially important in discussions,
in which speakers might have different attitudes about a topic.

You can often learn about a speaker's attitude from the sound of their voice.
When a speaker is expressing strong feelings, their voice often goes up and
down more than usual. Listen to the difference in the way the speaker says
this sentence:

🔊 5.3

I'm really surprised about that.

I'm really surprised about that. ↘

I'm really surprised about that! ↗

In the first sentence, the speaker's voice does not go up or down very much.
He does not have strong feelings.
In the second sentence, the speaker's voice goes down. He feels upset.
In the third sentence, the speaker's voice goes up. He feels excited.

5 🔊 5.4 Listen to the extracts. How do you think each speaker feels about
what they are saying? How do you know?

1 I'm really happy about this new research!
The speaker feels _____ . I know this because _____
_____ .

2 There's no question that happy people live longer.
The speaker feels _____ . I know this because _____
_____ .

3 It's ridiculous to get too worried about healthy eating and exercise!
The speaker feels _____ . I know this because _____
_____ .

4 He certainly never went to a gym.
The speaker feels _____ . I know this because _____
_____ .

5 There's no doubt that bad health habits increase the chances of getting
a serious illness.
The speaker feels _____ . I know this because _____
_____ .

Listening for attitude

You can also identify a speaker's attitude by listening for their use of:

Adjectives

A positive adjective used with a sarcastic intonation can express a negative attitude.

I'm afraid I lost your gym membership card.

*Well, that's just **great**!* (Great is usually a positive adjective, but here the speaker is not happy.)

Rhetorical questions

A rhetorical question (a question you are not expected to answer) is sometimes used to express a negative attitude.

So, you didn't enjoy the yoga class?

What do you think? (The rhetorical question makes it clear the speaker did not enjoy the class.)

But be careful! Rhetorical questions do not always express a negative attitude. Listen to the intonation to decide if the speaker has a negative attitude.

6 🔊 5.5 Work with a partner. Listen to the extracts and look at the audio script on page 215. Then, discuss the questions.

script on page 215.

1 Is the attitude of each speaker positive or negative?
2 What tells you their attitude – adjectives, rhetorical questions, intonation or a combination of these?

POST-LISTENING

Identifying references to common knowledge

Common knowledge means ideas which most people know about. Speakers often refer to common knowledge to make their arguments stronger and persuade other people that they are right. To express common knowledge, use phrases such as:

It's common knowledge that …   *There is no doubt that …*

Everyone knows that …   *Most people think that …*

There is no question that …

Sometimes speakers use these phrases with ideas which may not be completely true or which may not be shared by everyone, to persuade the listener that they are right.

7 Work with a partner. Look at the sentences. Do you agree with each statement? Why / Why not? Discuss your opinions.

1 **Most people think that** if they eat healthy food, they'll have a long, healthy life.
2 **There is no question that** happy people live longer.
3 **There is no doubt that** bad health habits increase the chances of getting a serious illness.
4 **Everyone knows that** exercise makes us happier.

DISCUSSION

8 Work with a partner. Discuss the questions.

1 Do you think your lifestyle is healthy? Why / Why not? What could you do to make your lifestyle healthier?
2 Do you know any very old, healthy people? What kind of lifestyle do they have?
3 If you want to have a healthy lifestyle, what do you think are the most important things to do?

9 Work with a partner. Do you agree or disagree with the statement below? Discuss your opinions and give reasons for them.

> There are more important things than a healthy lifestyle if you want to live a long life.

⊙ LANGUAGE DEVELOPMENT

PHRASAL VERBS

Phrasal verbs are two- or three-word verbs. They consist of a verb and one or two particles (small words like *up*, *out*, *in*). It is not always easy to understand the meaning of a phrasal verb by focusing only on the meaning of the verb and the particle(s). The parts together often have a completely different meaning than the individual parts.

When you see a phrasal verb that you do not know, try to work out its meaning from the context.

I **ran into** my old friend Henry at the gym. I was surprised to see him after so many years.

The words *surprised* and *see him* can help you figure out that the phrasal verb *run into* means *to meet someone you know when you are not expecting to*.

Phrasal verbs are very common in informal, spoken English. Try to memorize any new phrasal verbs and use them when you speak.

1 Look at the sentences. Underline the phrasal verb in each sentence.

1 If you want to lose weight, you should <u>cut down on</u> fatty foods.
2 Last winter, I came down with four colds. I hope I'm healthier this year!
3 I want to try something new. Maybe I'll take up tennis.
4 Tim is going to try out for the football team. I don't think he'll make it, though – he's not a great player.
5 No matter how good their genes are, these children will not be able to enjoy a long and happy life unless they give up crisps, chocolate bars and sugary drinks.
6 Why don't you sign up for a yoga class? Yoga is good exercise and it helps you relax.
7 Would you like to join in the game? You can be on our team.
8 It took me a long time to get over the flu. I was ill for two weeks.

2 Work with a partner. Discuss the questions.

1 What do you think the phrasal verbs in Exercise 1 mean?
2 What words in the context helped you work out the meanings?

PLUS

3 Write the phrasal verbs from Exercise 1 next to the correct definitions.

1 _____ to get an illness, especially one which is not serious
2 _____ to stop a habit, often because it is unhealthy
3 _____ to agree to become involved in an organized activity
4 _____ to become involved in an activity with other people
5 _____ to compete for a position on a sports team or a part in a play
6 _____ to become healthy again after having an illness
7 _____ to start doing a particular job or activity
8 _____ to eat or drink less of something

4 Complete the questions with phrasal verbs.

1 Have you ever _____ a bad habit, like eating chocolate?
2 Have you ever had a cold or the flu? How long did it take you to _____ it?
3 Have you ever _____ for exercise classes or for a gym membership?
4 Have you _____ any new activities in the past few years?
5 Have you ever _____ for a team?
6 Are there any foods which you want to _____ ? Why do you want to eat less of these foods?

5 Write a follow-up question for each of the questions in Exercise 4.

1 What did you give up? _____
2 _____
3 _____
4 _____
5 _____
6 _____

6 Work with a partner. Ask and answer the questions in Exercise 4. Ask your follow-up questions to find out more information.

Have you ever given up a bad habit, like eating chocolate?

Yes, I have.

What did you give up?

I gave up fast food. Burgers, chips, that sort of thing!

ADJECTIVES TO DESCRIBE WELL-BEING

7 Read the definitions. Complete the sentences with the words in bold.

> **cultural** (adj) relating to the habits, traditions and beliefs of a society
> **educational** (adj) relating to learning
> **emotional** (adj) relating to feelings
> **intellectual** (adj) relating to your ability to think and understand things, especially complicated ideas
> **personal** (adj) relating to a single person rather than to a group
> **physical** (adj) relating to the body
> **social** (adj) relating to activities in which you meet and spend time with other people

1 Exercising has _____ benefits. It can make you happier and calmer.
2 If you want to improve your _____ life, you should join a club to meet some new people.
3 Andrea is very _____ . She enjoys talking about literature and philosophy.
4 Max wanted to learn Spanish quickly, so he hired a _____ tutor. He meets with his tutor twice a week for conversation practice.
5 _____ activity helps your body stay strong and healthy.
6 When you move to a new country, it can take some time to get used to the _____ differences.
7 Travel is fun and it's also _____ . You can learn a lot about the history and culture of other places when you travel.

PLUS

PREPARING TO LISTEN

1 You are going to listen to four presentations about programmes which can improve your health. Before you listen, circle the best definition for each word in bold.

1 I don't feel like going to the gym this afternoon. I just want to stay at home, **relax** and watch a film.
   a to sleep until later than usual
   b to study for a test
   c to become less tense or worried

2 Marcus is feeling a lot of **stress** at work. It's giving him headaches.
   a worry caused by a difficult situation
   b an illness caused by not getting enough sleep
   c energy you get from interacting with people

3 Drinking a lot of water can be a good **treatment** for a stomachache.
   a a solution to a problem
   b a way to cure an illness or injury
   c something you can drink

4 If you **reduce** the number of calories you eat, you will lose weight.
   a to count the amount of something
   b to make (something) less in size, amount, etc.
   c to make (something) larger in size, amount, etc.

5 Exercise has a number of **mental** benefits, like improving memory.
   a relating to the mind
   b relating to movement
   c relating to exercise

6 Eating healthy food can improve your athletic **performance**. It makes your muscles and bones stronger and helps you stay healthy.
   a how often a person does an activity
   b how well a person does an activity
   c how often a person wins

7 Writing requires a lot of **concentration**. It's a good idea to be alone in a quiet room when you're writing.
   a the energy required to do something
   b the ability to stay calm for long periods of time
   c the ability to give your whole attention to one thing

8 Anyone can **participate** in the game. You don't need to be an experienced player to join.
   a to be involved in an activity
   b to do something well
   c to stop doing something

PLUS

2 Work with a partner. Look at the photos. What do you think are the benefits – if any – of each activity? Discuss your ideas.

taekwondo

_____
_____
_____

team sports

_____
_____
_____

cycling

_____
_____
_____

acupuncture
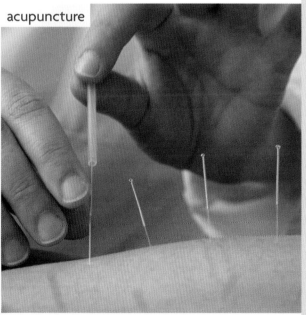

_____
_____
_____

LISTENING FOR MAIN IDEAS

3 🔊 5.6 Listen to the four presentations. What is each one describing?

a cycling tour   acupuncture   a football club   taekwondo

Presentation 1: _____

Presentation 2: _____

Presentation 3: _____

Presentation 4: _____

4 🔊 5.6 Listen again. What are the benefits of each programme? Take notes.

TAKING NOTES ON DETAIL

Benefits of the health programmes

Programme 1:

Programme 2:

Programme 3:

Programme 4:

DISCUSSION

SYNTHESIZING

5 Work in small groups. Use ideas from Listening 1 and Listening 2 to answer the following questions.

1 What do you think each speaker in Listening 1 would think about the programmes in Listening 2? Why?

2 Do you still agree with your answer to this question from the start of the unit?

What advice would you give to someone who wants to live to be 100 years old? What should the person do or not do?

3 Do you want to try any of the activities in the presentations in Listening 2? Which ones? Why / Why not?

CRITICAL THINKING

At the end of this unit, you will do the speaking task below.

Give a presentation to a group of students about an idea for a health product or programme.

SKILLS

Brainstorming and evaluating ideas using an ideas map

Ideas maps are a good way to organize your notes as you listen. They help you see connections between the topic, the main ideas and the details.

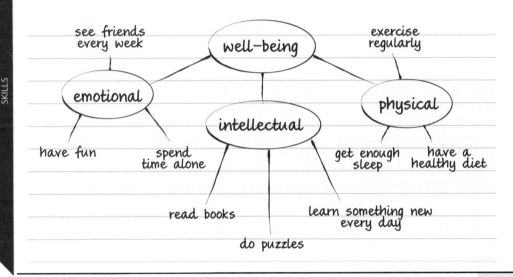

1 Choose one of the programmes from Listening 2 and complete the ideas map.

UNDERSTAND

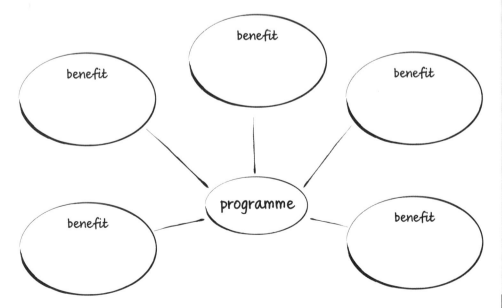

2 Work in groups. Brainstorm ideas for different health-related programmes which you might like to talk about. Write your ideas in the ideas map.

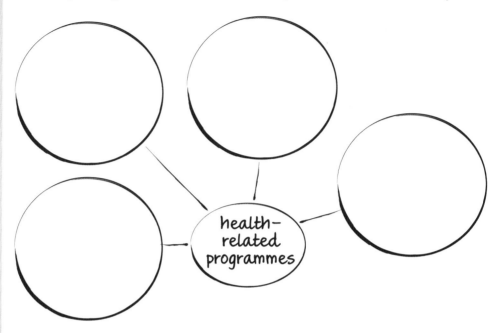

3 Look at the health programmes you brainstormed in Exercise 2. Which has the most health benefits? Which has the fewest? Why? Choose one and write it in the centre of the ideas map below.

4 Think of some benefits of the programme you are going to talk about and write them on the outside circles of the ideas map.

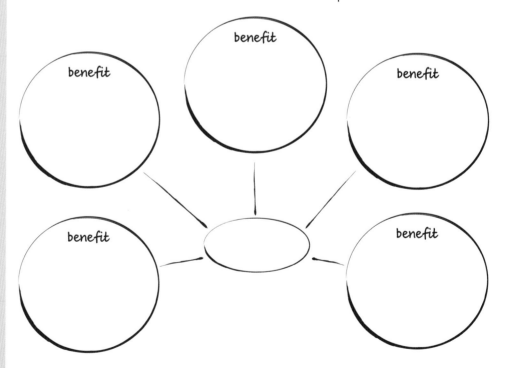

PREPARATION FOR SPEAKING

PROBLEM–SOLUTION ORGANIZATION

1 Work with a partner. Look at the script for a presentation about a programme below and discuss the questions.

  1 Why does the script begin with rhetorical questions?
  _____

  2 Why are all the rhetorical questions *yes/no* questions about *you*?
  _____

  3 What three problems do the questions introduce?
  _____
  _____
  _____

  4 What is the solution to the problems?
  _____

  5 What is the purpose of the part of the script that begins 'And as we all know'?
  _____

  6 What does the script say the programme is good for?
  _____

  7 What information does the last part of the script provide?
  _____

2 What is the organization of the presentation? Number the information.

  • specific information about the place, time, etc. _____
  • background information about the programme _____
  • rhetorical questions about the problems, to attract the listeners' attention ___1___
  • introduction of the solution _____

Script for presentation

Do you have problems focusing on your work? Are you under a lot of stress? Do you want to get more exercise while trying something new and exciting? If so, it's time to take up taekwondo! Taekwondo is great exercise. And as we all know, exercise improves your health. Taekwondo also has mental benefits – it has been shown to improve your concentration. In addition, it makes you feel good about yourself. This martial art was developed in Korea, and is now popular around the world. Whether you are looking for physical well-being, increased confidence or a life with less stress, Black Belt taekwondo club has it all. Sign up now for a free introductory class, starting on January 15th.

PRESENTING PERSUASIVELY

Speakers often try to persuade listeners to agree with them or to take action. Using rhetorical questions and identifying common knowledge are common persuasive techniques. Other persuasive techniques include:

1 **Using the imperative form.** The imperative form of a verb is strong and direct, so it is effective for persuasion. It is often used in advertisements.
Join us and take advantage of the many benefits of team sports.

2 **Using adjectives.** Adjectives help to persuade people by making them feel emotions.
So be kind to your body and your mind and come with us on an amazing adventure you'll never forget!

3 Look at the extracts from the presentations. Underline the imperative verb forms.

   1 <u>Sign up</u> now for a free introductory class, starting on January 15th.
   2 If you're interested in learning more about our group, check out our website at www.footballsundays.cup.com.
   3 This spring, join our six-month course in acupuncture.
   4 Learn more about the course and visit us on our open days on the first Saturday of every month.

4 Work with a partner. Answer the questions.

   1 What effect do the imperatives have on the listener?

      _____

   2 Why are imperatives used in the presentations?

      _____
      _____

5 Make the sentences more persuasive by using imperative verb forms.

   1 If you want, you can buy our new product.
     Buy our new product!
   2 It is possible to buy one and get one free.

      _____

   3 You should hurry and purchase a ticket now.

      _____

   4 People must not forget that our shops are open on Sundays.

      _____

   5 We would like you to register for our course before it's too late!

      _____

6 Look at the extracts. Underline the adjectives.

1 Do you want to get more exercise while trying something new and exciting?

2 Would you like to improve your social life, your intellectual performance, your physical fitness and your team-building skills?

3 Not only does this trip provide terrific exercise and a fascinating cultural experience, it's the best way to learn.

4 Are you interested in alternative treatments?

5 Have you ever wanted to explore the secrets of traditional Chinese medicine?

6 It's also a great alternative for people who want to lose weight in an easy way.

7 Work with a partner. Discuss the questions.

1 Do the adjectives in Exercise 6 have a positive or negative meaning?

_____

2 What images come to mind when you hear these adjectives?

_____

_____

3 Think of other adjectives you often hear in advertisements and persuasive presentations. Look at Exercise 5 again. Write a second sentence using a positive adjective.

Buy our new product! It's amazing.

SPEAKING TASK

▶ Give a presentation to a group of students about an idea for a health product or programme.

PREPARE

1 Look at the ideas map you created in Exercise 4 in the Critical thinking section. Review your notes and add any new information.

2 Make notes about what you will say. Use this organization:

1 rhetorical questions to introduce the problem and attract the listener's attention

2 introduction of the product or programme and explanation of how it solves the problem

3 background information about the product or programme

4 specific details about the place, time and/or costs

3 Make a list of adjectives you will use to describe your product or programme.

4 Make notes about common knowledge which you can use to help persuade your audience. You can use language like this:

It's common knowledge that ...   There is no question that ...
Everyone knows that ...   Most people think that ...
There is no doubt that ...

5 Refer to the Task checklist below as you prepare your presentation.

TASK CHECKLIST	✔
Use phrasal verbs correctly.	
Use adjectives to describe well-being correctly.	
Use problem–solution organization correctly.	
Use imperatives to persuade the listener.	
Use adjectives to persuade the listener.	

PRACTISE

6 Work in small groups. Take turns practising your presentations.
Take notes on your classmates' presentations and feed back to them on how persuasive it was.

PRESENT

7 Take turns giving your presentations to the class.

OBJECTIVES REVIEW

1 Check your learning objectives for this unit. Write *3*, *2* or *1* for each objective.

3 = very well   2 = well   1 = not so well

I can ...

watch and understand a video about tackling the problem of obesity in children. _____

listen for attitude. _____

identify references to common knowledge. _____

brainstorm and evaluate ideas using an ideas map. _____

understand and use phrasal verbs. _____

use problem–solution organization. _____

present persuasively. _____

give a presentation to a group of students about an idea for a health product or programme. _____

2 Go to the *Unlock* Online Workbook for more practice with this unit's learning objectives.

UNL○CK
ONLINE

WORDLIST

come down with (phr v)	intellectual (adj) ⊙	relax (v)
concentration (n) ⊙	join in (phr v)	sign up for (phr v)
cultural (adj) ⊙	mental (adj) ⊙	social (adj) ⊙
cut down on (phr v)	overweight (adj)	stress (n)
educational (adj) ⊙	participate (v) ⊙	take up (phr v)
emotional (adj) ⊙	performance (n) ⊙	treatment (n) ⊙
get over (phr v)	personal (adj) ⊙	try out for (phr v)
give up (phr v)	physical (adj) ⊙	unhealthy (adj)
habit (n) ⊙	prove (v) ⊙	work out (phr v)
illness (n) ⊙	reduce (v) ⊙	

⊙ = high-frequency words in the Cambridge Academic Corpus

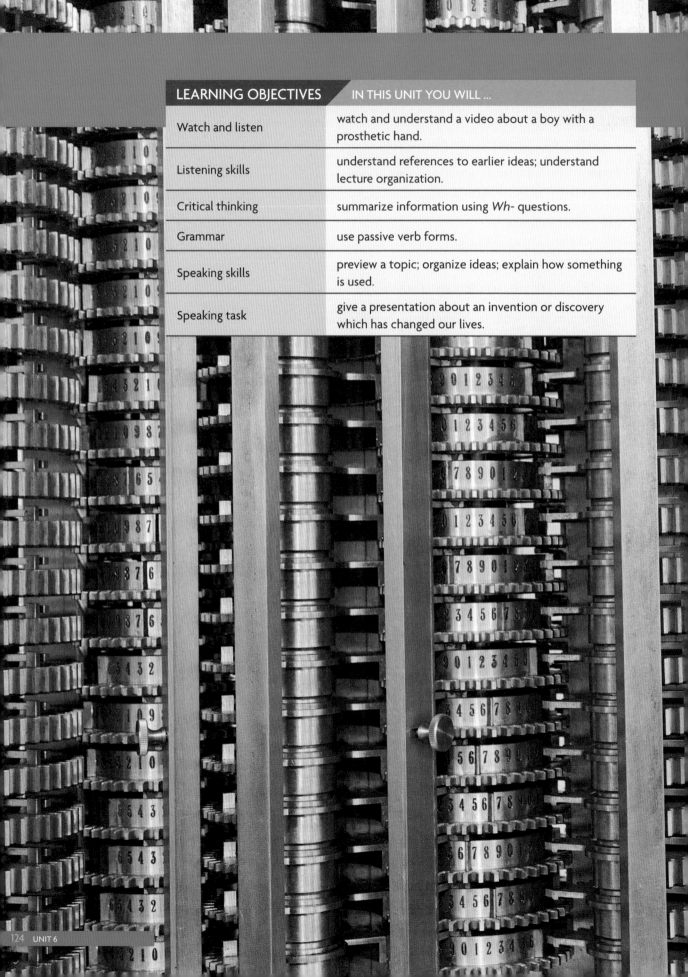

LEARNING OBJECTIVES

IN THIS UNIT YOU WILL ...

Watch and listen	watch and understand a video about a boy with a prosthetic hand.
Listening skills	understand references to earlier ideas; understand lecture organization.
Critical thinking	summarize information using *Wh-* questions.
Grammar	use passive verb forms.
Speaking skills	preview a topic; organize ideas; explain how something is used.
Speaking task	give a presentation about an invention or discovery which has changed our lives.

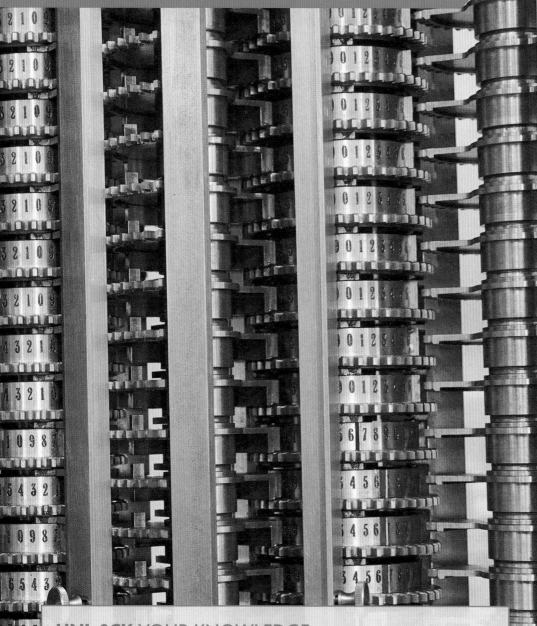

DISCOVERY AND INVENTION

UNL🔓CK YOUR KNOWLEDGE

Work with a partner. Discuss the questions.

1 The photo shows a very early computer. When do you think it was invented?

2 What famous inventions or discoveries come from your country?

3 What do you think is the most important invention or discovery in the last 20 years? Why is it important?

PLUS

WATCH AND LISTEN

PREPARING TO WATCH

1 Work with a partner. Discuss the questions.

1 What can we make with 3D printers? Are these things expensive?
2 Why do some people need artificial body parts or prosthetic replacements?
3 Can you think of any famous people with prosthetic replacements?

2 Work with a partner. Look at the photos from the video and discuss the questions.

1 What can the boy do with the prosthetic hand?
2 How do you think the boy feels about the hand?
3 What role does the college student in the fourth photo play in this situation?

GLOSSARY

device (n) a piece of equipment which is used for a particular purpose

prosthetic replacement (n phr) an artificial body part, for example, one which takes the place of an arm or foot

wrist (n) the part of your body between your hand and your arm

grip (n) a tight, strong hold on something, usually with your hand

take for granted (idm) to expect something and not understand that you are lucky to have it

pay off (phr v) to bring success, especially after hard work and a period of time

crowdfunding (n) collecting money for a particular purpose from a large group of people, often by asking for help on the internet

WHILE WATCHING

3 ▶ Watch the video. Complete the paragraph with the words in the box.

3D   college   expensive   new   normal   prosthetic   successful

Holden Mora is showing the reporter his [1]_____ hand. Normally, a hand like this would be very [2]_____ – but a [3]_____ student made this one for $20 using a [4]_____ printer. He wanted Holden to be able to do [5]_____ things like hold a bottle or a knife and fork. The project was so [6]_____ that 11 other children are now waiting for their [7]_____ hands.

4 ▶ Watch the video again. Correct the sentences.

1 Holden Mora is 17 years old.

_____

2 Jeff Powell built the hand using instructions from his professor.

_____

3 The printer builds the parts in under 44 hours.

_____

4 Holden cannot hold things with his artificial hand.

_____

5 Holden is now raising money to build hands for other kids.

_____

6 Holden hopes other teachers can have the best kind of hands, too.

_____

DISCUSSION

5 Work in small groups. Discuss the questions. Then, compare your answers with another group.

1 Think of something in your life which was physically very difficult for you to do. How did you learn to do it?

2 Are you surprised by how happy and excited the boy in the video is? Why / Why not?

3 What other ways could 3D printers be used to help people?

LISTENING

LISTENING 1

PREPARING TO LISTEN

1 You are going to listen to a museum tour about inventions from the Middle Ages. Before you listen, read the words and their definitions below. Complete the sentences with the correct form of the words in bold.

> **design** (v) to make or draw plans for something
> **develop** (v) to make something over a period of time
> **device** (n) a piece of equipment which is used for a particular purpose
> **diagram** (n) a simple picture which shows how something works or what it looks like
> **discover** (v) to find information, a place or an object, especially for the first time
> **invent** (v) to create something which had never been made before
> **scientific** (adj) relating to the study of science
> **technology** (n) knowledge, equipment and methods used in science and industry

1 Al-Jazari _____ machines to help with farming. He made drawings and gave detailed descriptions of how to build these machines.
2 _____ research has proven that genes can affect our health.
3 Scientists hope to someday _____ a cure for cancer.
4 The Chinese _____ gunpowder and used it for fireworks.
5 A baby monitor is a _____ which lets parents watch their baby when they're in a different room.
6 It can often take many years to _____ a new drug.
7 This _____ isn't very clear. I can't figure out how to put this together!
8 Modern _____ , such as computers and mobile phones, has changed our lives.

2 Match the photos to the inventions. When do you think they were invented?

1 the fountain pen _____
2 glasses _____
3 gunpowder _____
4 the crankshaft _____

a

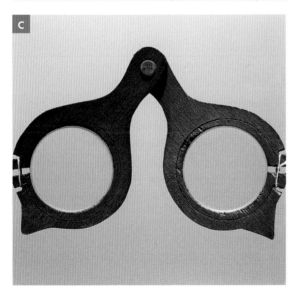

b

c

d

WHILE LISTENING

3 🔊 6.1 Listen to a museum tour which mentions the inventions from Exercise 2. Number the inventions in the order they are mentioned.

the fountain pen _____
glasses _____
gunpowder _____
the crankshaft _____

4 🔊 6.1 Complete the notes with as much information as you can remember. Then, listen to the tour again to check your notes and add more details.

invention	when it was invented	where it was invented	who invented it	why it was invented
fountain (1)_____	(2)_____	(3)_____	unknown	so people wouldn't get (4)_____ on their fingers
(5)_____	(6)_____ century	(7)_____	unknown	to help people (8)_____
crankshaft	(9)_____ century	(10)_____	al-Jazari, a great (11)_____	to water (12)_____ and fields on (13)_____ (now used in (14)_____ engines)
gunpowder	(15)_____ century	(16)_____	(17)_____	to try to (18)_____ forever

POST-LISTENING

Understanding references to earlier ideas

To refer to things they talked about earlier, speakers often use words such as *it, he, she, they, then* and *there*. This sounds more natural than repeating the same words. In this sentence, the word *it* refers back to the invention of the telephone:

In 1876, Bell invented <u>the telephone</u>. ← It changed the way we communicate.

5 Look at the sentences. Underline the words which the words in bold refer to.

1 The first fountain pen was made in 953 in Africa. Before **then**, people used bird feathers and ink to write with.

2 As some of you may know, the Middle Ages have often been called the 'Dark Ages'. During this tour, you will find out that **they** were not.

3 Glasses were invented in Italy in the thirteenth century. No one knows who invented **them**.

4 The invention of gunpowder has changed the way we fight wars. **It** changed the outcome of many medieval battles and affected the history of the world.

PRONUNCIATION FOR LISTENING

SKILLS

Weak and strong forms

In spoken English, small words (such as *a, an, the, do, does, to, from, at, of*) are not usually stressed. When these words are unstressed, they are called *weak forms*.

The unstressed vowel in these weak forms is pronounced /ə/ (*to* = /tə/, *the* = /ðə/, etc.).

However, speakers sometimes stress these small words to make them the main part of their message. When these words are stressed, they are called *strong forms*.

Andrea is funny **and** intelligent. (The speaker is stressing that Andrea has both of these qualities.)

---

6 🔊 6.2 Listen for the weak forms and complete the sentences.

1 Inventions _____ technology from India, China, North Africa, _____ _____ Middle East were brought _____ Europe.

2 _____ first glasses were held in front _____ eyes or balanced on _____ nose.

3 _____ crankshaft is _____ long arm which allows machines _____ move _____ _____ straight line.

4 As we move along, you'll find one _____ _____ most important inventions _____ medieval times.

7 🔊 6.3 Listen to the extracts. Match the extracts 1–3 to the reasons for using strong forms (a–c).

1 The Middle Ages **were** an interesting time and they were full of scientific discoveries. _____

2 Inventions and machines designed by medieval scholars made a great contribution to society and many are still in use today. **And** some of these inventions are very common. _____

3 Many people think gunpowder is **the** most important invention in history. _____

Strong forms are used ...

a to emphasize that there is nothing better or more than this.

b to contrast with an earlier idea that the Middle Ages were **not** an interesting time.

c to emphasize that there is more information.

DISCUSSION

8 Look at the photos of some Chinese inventions. Think about the questions and make notes.

1 How do you think these inventions changed people's lives?
2 Are these inventions still used? How?
3 Which invention do you think is the most important? Why?

9 Work in a group. Take turns explaining why the invention you chose is the most important.

PLUS

the compass

making paper

printing

⊙ LANGUAGE DEVELOPMENT

USES OF THE VERB *MAKE*

The verb *make* has three main meanings: *force*, *cause* or *produce*.

Force: My boss **made** me work late last night.

Cause: Water and weights **make** the mechanical clocks work.

Produce: The first fountain pen was **made** in 953.

Make is also used in phrases with many nouns. These include:

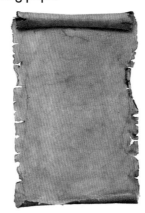

an attempt
a contribution   an investment

a comparison —— make

                              progress

a decision
                    public
        a difference

VOCABULARY

1 Look at the sentences. What is the meaning of *make* in each sentence? Write *C* (cause), *F* (force) or *P* (produce).

1 Gunpowder was first **made** in China. __P__

2 My professor **made** me rewrite my assignment because there were too many mistakes. _____

3 Social media **makes** it easy for people to stay in touch. _____

4 Today, most pens are **made** of plastic. _____

5 The new discovery **made** a lot of people very happy. _____

6 I **made** myself stay up late to finish the work. _____

2 Circle the best definition for each phrase in bold.

1 If you **make a comparison** between these two TVs, you'll see that this one has a much clearer picture.
   a to consider the benefits of something
   b to consider the similarities between two things

2 I like both of these phones a lot. It's hard to **make a decision** about which one to buy.
   a to choose
   b to know

3 Inventions and machines designed by medieval scholars **made a** great **contribution** to society.
   a to give money in order to support a good cause, e.g. a charity
   b to help to make something successful

4 The invention of the light bulb **made a** huge **difference** in people's lifestyles. After it was invented, life was never the same.
   a to remove something
   b to improve something

5 For over a century, inventors have been **making attempts** to create a car which can fly, but they haven't succeeded.
   a to try
   b to fail

6 About ten years ago, Andrew **made a** smart **investment** in a tech start-up company and now he's a millionaire.
   a to start a small business
   b to put money into something to make a profit

7 This is a good smartphone, but they could still **make improvements** to it. For example, I wish it had longer battery life.
   a to make something better
   b to make something more expensive

8 The company announced that it's going to be taken over, but the identity of the buyer won't be **made public** until later this month.
   a to share information about something
   b to make a presentation about something

PLUS

PASSIVE VERB FORMS

In an *active sentence* we focus on who or what did something. In a *passive sentence* the focus is on what happened to someone or something. To form the past simple of the passive, use *was / were* + past participle.

Active: **Alan Turing** <u>invented</u> the digital computer. (focus on the inventor)
Passive: **The digital computer** <u>was invented</u> in 1936. (focus on the invention)
Passive: **Digital computers** <u>were invented</u> in 1936. (focus on the invention)
Use *by* with the passive when it is also important to know who did something.
The digital computer <u>was invented</u> in 1936 **by** Alan Turing.

3 Look at the extracts from Listening 1. Underline the eight passive verb forms.

1 The Middle Ages were an interesting time, and they were full of scientific discoveries. During this time, inventions and technology from India, China, North Africa and the Middle East were brought to Europe.

2 And some of these inventions are very common. For example, the first fountain pen was made in 953 in Africa. Before then, people used bird feathers and ink to write with.

3 Glasses were invented in Italy in the thirteenth century. No one knows who invented them. The first glasses were held in front of the eyes or balanced on the nose. They were developed to help people with bad vision to read.

4 However, his most important invention was the crankshaft. The crankshaft is a long arm which allows machines to move in a straight line. It was first used for watering gardens and fields on farms.

5 Gunpowder was invented in the ninth century by Chinese scientists who were trying to create a powder which would make you live forever. They weren't successful, of course, but their attempts led to the invention of fireworks and weapons. The first instructions on how to make gunpowder were written in the eleventh century by Zeng Gongliang, Ding Du and Yang Weide.

PLUS

4 Work with a partner. Write each sentence in the passive form.

1 Apple's first tablet computer – develop – the 1990s
   <u>Apple's first tablet computer was developed in the 1990s.</u>

2 the law of gravity – discover – Isaac Newton – the seventeenth century
   _____

3 the first computer chip – invent – the 1950s
   _____

4 the first smartphone – create – after 1997
   _____

5 penicillin – first discover – 1928 – Alexander Fleming
   _____

5 Complete the sentences using the correct form of the verbs in brackets. Use active or passive forms.

1 Paper _____ (discover) in ancient China.

2 The telephone _____ (invent) in 1876.

3 Imhotep, an Egyptian architect, _____ (design) the pyramid of Djoser.

4 Glasses _____ (develop) to help people with bad vision to read.

5 This letter _____ (write) with a fountain pen.

6 A very early calculator _____ (create) by Blaise Pascal.

7 Millions of people _____ (download) smartphone apps every day.

8 The pictures _____ (send) by email.

9 The first photograph _____ (take) around 1826.

10 Edison _____ (develop) his first light bulb in 1879.

6 Find and correct the verb errors in the sentences. (Tip: One sentence does not have an error.) Then, check your answers with a partner.

1 The first smartphone, Simon, were created by IBM.

_____

2 DNA is discovered by James Watson and Francis Crick in the 1950s.

_____

3 The first newspaper was print in 1605 in Germany.

_____

4 The first computer program was wrote by Ada Lovelace.

_____

5 Hearing aids were developed to help people hear better.

_____

6 Margaret Knight was invented the paper bag in 1868.

_____

7 Work with a partner. What do you know about the inventions mentioned in Exercises 4, 5 and 6?

PREPARING TO LISTEN

UNDERSTANDING KEY VOCABULARY

1 You are going to listen to a lecture about the history of smartphone apps. Before you listen, read the definitions. Complete the sentences with the correct form of the words in bold.

> **access** (v) to be able to enter or use something
> **allow** (v) to make it possible for someone to do something
> **app** (n) (abbreviation for *application*) software designed for a particular purpose which you can download onto a smartphone or other mobile device
> **create** (v) to make something new or invent something
> **industry** (n) the companies and activities involved in the process of producing goods for sale
> **install** (v) to put new software onto a computer or mobile device
> **product** (n) something which is made to be sold
> **users** (n) people who use a product, machine or service

1 I need a password to _____ the Wi-Fi connection in this café.
2 Once you download the _____ , you have to _____ it on your smartphone.
3 This software lets you _____ your own apps. I have some great ideas I'd like to try!
4 In a recent study, 45% of American smartphone _____ said they would rather give up their holidays than their phone.
5 I always read _____ reviews before I buy an expensive item.
6 IT (information technology) is an extremely fast-growing _____ .
7 Smartphones _____ us to stay in touch with each other constantly.

USING YOUR KNOWLEDGE

2 Work in small groups and discuss the questions.

1 Approximately how many apps do you have on your phone? How often do you install new ones? Which apps do you use most often? Are there any which you never use?
2 How many apps do you think are downloaded every year worldwide?
3 How have smartphones and apps changed people's lives?

WHILE LISTENING

3 🔊 6.4 Listen to an introduction to a lecture. Number the topics in the order that they will be discussed.

   a The influence of apps on our lives _____

   b Specific examples of popular apps _____

   c The history of apps _____

4 Make a list of the five types of smartphone apps which you think are the most useful.

   1 ☐ _____   4 ☐ _____

   2 ☐ _____   5 ☐ _____

   3 ☐ _____

5 🔊 6.5 Listen to the lecture. Tick the types of apps you listed in Exercise 4 which the speaker mentioned.

6 🔊 6.5 Complete the notes below in as much detail as you can. Then, listen to the lecture again to check your notes and add more details.

first apps used for:
- accessing the (1)_____
- (2)_____
- (3)_____

second gen. apps:
- (4)_____ opened in 2008
- 2011 – 10 billion downloads
     - people used apps more than (5)_____
- by 2017 – (6)_____ downloads

road trip before smartphones: (7)_____

road trip after smartphones: (8)_____

another effect of apps:
- there is a need for skilled (9)_____

negative effects of apps:
- people are more (10)_____
- people are less (11)_____

POST-LISTENING

Understanding lecture organization

Lecturers often use special phrases to help the audience follow the lecture. In the introduction, they explain what they'll talk about and in what order. They use language such as:

First, we'll discuss ...   I'd like to start by talking about ...

They also use special expressions to show transitions from one topic to another. They use language such as:

Next, I will discuss ...   Now I'd like to talk about ...

LISTENING FOR TEXT ORGANIZATION

7 Look at the extracts from the lecture. Underline the expressions the lecturer uses to say what will happen next.

1 <u>We'll start by</u> discussing the very first apps and their development.
2 We will then discuss how apps have changed our lives.
3 I'd like to start by talking a little bit about the first apps.
4 I'm going to briefly talk about how these apps have changed our lives.
5 Now I'd like to mention another important effect of the invention of apps.
6 In the next part of the lecture, I'll discuss some of the most common apps in more detail.

DISCUSSION

SYNTHESIZING

8 Work in small groups. Use ideas from Listening 1 and Listening 2 to answer the following questions.

1 Think about your answer to Exercise 9 on page 132. Do you think the invention of the smartphone is more important than the invention you chose? Why / Why not?
2 If you could invent anything (including an app), what would you invent? Why?
3 Technology has developed rapidly in the last century. Do you think its development is slowing now? Why / Why not?
4 What do you think will be the most important invention in the next 25 years?

SPEAKING

CRITICAL THINKING

At the end of this unit, you will do the speaking task below.

> Give a presentation about an invention or discovery which has changed our lives.

Summarizing information using *Wh-* questions

When you do research on a topic, try asking yourself the following questions: *Who? What? When? Where? Why?* Many researchers add *How?* to this list. Then, search for the answers to these questions. To organize your research, it is helpful to make an ideas map like the one in Exercise 1. This is a quick and easy way to focus on the key details of a topic.

UNDERSTAND

1 Choose one of the inventions from Listening 1 or one of the apps from Listening 2. Write this in the middle of the circle below. Complete the ideas map for the invention. Use information from your notes on page 130 or 137. Try answering some of these questions:

1 When was the last time you used this thing?
2 What are its uses?
3 What would life be like without it?
4 How has it affected our lives?

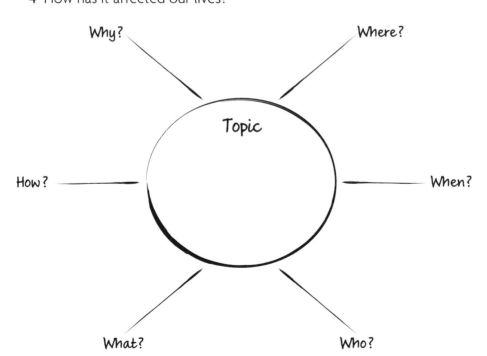

2 Work with a partner. Share your ideas maps. Make suggestions about information which your partner could add.

3 Choose an invention to talk about in the speaking task. You can talk about one of the inventions in the photos below or use your own idea.

the credit card

the microwave

the refrigerator

the car

4 Complete an ideas map about the invention you chose.

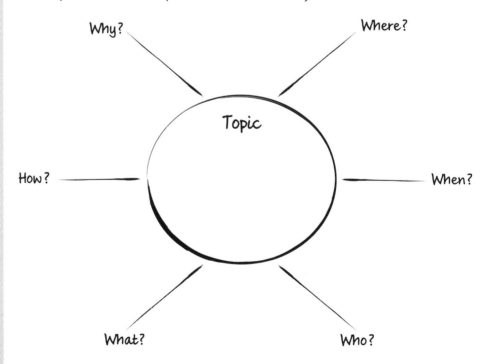

5 Work with a partner. Share your ideas maps. Make suggestions about information which your partner could add.

PREPARATION FOR SPEAKING

PREVIEWING A TOPIC

SKILLS

> In the introduction to a presentation, give a preview of what you will talk about. This helps your audience follow your talk. Here are some examples of language you can use to preview a topic:
>
> I'd like to begin my talk by looking at ...
> After that, I'm going to explain ...
> Then, I'll discuss ...
> Finally, I'll explore ...

1 🔊 6.6 Listen to an introduction to a presentation which previews what the speaker will talk about. Tick the things that the speaker does.

1 ☐ mentions the invention's name in the first sentence
2 ☐ gives a description of the invention
3 ☐ says how you can use it
4 ☐ gives specific details of how it was invented
5 ☐ explains what will happen next in the presentation

2 Work with a partner. Practise giving an introduction about a simple invention. Use the preview below to organize your ideas.

Student A: give an introduction to a presentation about the **plastic bag**.

Student B: give an introduction to a presentation about the **ballpoint pen**.

> I would like to present an invention which has changed the way we
> _____ . It's a simple invention and we have all used it.
> It's the _____ .
> A _____ is _____ .
> (explain the invention here)
> You can _____ .
> (explain how it is used in general)
> First, I am going to talk about _____ . Then, I will
> explain how it has improved our lives.

ORGANIZING IDEAS

Before you write a presentation outline, decide in what order you will present your ideas. First, brainstorm some ideas and write them down. Then, put them in order to create the framework for your outline. This will help you make sure that your ideas are in a logical order when you start writing. For example, it is logical to tell your listeners background information before you tell them why something is useful. You can use *Wh-* questions to organize your presentation.

3 Read the next part of the presentation. Number the questions a–g in the order they are answered in the presentation.

   a Why do people use them? _____
   b Who invented them? _____
   c Where can people use them? _____
   d Why were they invented? _____
   e When were they invented? __1__
   f What is the best thing about the invention? _____
   g When were they first sold? _____

To start with, Post-it® notes were invented in 1974 by Art Fry. Fry needed a bookmark which would stay inside the book and didn't fall out. He used a special type of glue invented by his colleague Spencer Silver. The glue was not very strong and made it easy to remove the notes.

In 1977, the first Post-it® notes were sold in shops. Since then, they have become a global phenomenon. People all over the word recognize the small, yellow sticky notes. We use them at work, at school and at home.

Because the glue does not leave any stains, people can stick Post-it® notes to anything. They allow us to remember important information and take notes. The best thing is that you can stick a Post-it® note anywhere to help you remember something.

EXPLAINING HOW SOMETHING IS USED

We can use the words and expressions in bold to talk about how something is used.

Post-it® notes **help people to** remember things.

Without the crankshaft, car engines wouldn't work.

The microwave **makes it** possible to cook food quickly.

Social media **is useful for** communicating with friends.

The light bulb **allows us to** see at night.

4 Complete the sentences with phrases from the box.

| allows us   are useful for   helps people to   makes it   without |

1 GPS _____ to find our way around unknown places.
2 The mobile phone _____ stay in touch.
3 Translation apps _____ learning another language.
4 Television _____ easy to learn about the world.
5 _____ the computer chip, we wouldn't be able to use laptops.

5 Write two sentences about the laptop computer and two sentences about the smartphone. Use phrases from Exercise 4.

laptop

_____
_____

smartphone

_____
_____

6 Work with a partner. Take turns saying your sentences.

Laptops allow us to work at home more easily.

Smartphones make it easy to share photos and videos.

SPEAKING TASK

▸ Give a presentation about an invention or discovery which has changed our lives.

PREPARE

1 Look at the ideas map you created in Exercise 4 in the Critical thinking section. Review your notes and add any new information. Decide in what order you will answer the *Wh-* questions. Write the questions in order below.

1 _____

2 _____

3 _____

4 _____

5 _____

6 _____

2 Make notes about the language you will use. Use language like:

To preview your topic
I'd like to start by talking about ...
Then, I'll discuss ...
After that, I'm going to explain ...
Finally, I'll explore ...

To explain how something is used
_____ helps people to ...
Without _____ , ...
_____ makes it _____ to ...
_____ is useful for ...

3 Refer to the Task checklist below as you prepare your presentation.

TASK CHECKLIST	✔
Use phrases with *make* correctly.	
Preview the topic clearly.	
Organize your ideas in a logical order.	
Explain clearly how something is used.	

PRACTISE

4 Work with a partner. Take turns practising your presentation.

PRESENT

5 Work in small groups. Take turns giving your presentations. Discuss which one of your inventions or discoveries has had the biggest influence on our lives.

OBJECTIVES REVIEW

1 Check your learning objectives for this unit. Write *3, 2* or *1* for each objective.

3 = very well   2 = well   1 = not so well

I can ...

watch and understand a video about a boy with a prosthetic hand. _____

understand references to earlier ideas. _____

understand lecture organization. _____

summarize information using *Wh-* questions. _____

use passive verb forms. _____

preview a topic. _____

organize ideas. _____

explain how something is used. _____

give a presentation about an invention or discovery which has changed our lives. _____

2 Go to the *Unlock* Online Workbook for more practice with this unit's learning objectives.

 UNLOCK
ONLINE

WORDLIST

access (v) ⊙	discover (v) ⊙	make an investment (v phr)
allow (v) ⊙	industry (n) ⊙	make attempts (v phr)
app (n)	install (v)	make improvements (v phr)
create (v) ⊙	invent (v)	make public (v phr)
design (v) ⊙	make a comparison (v phr)	product (n) ⊙
develop (v) ⊙	make a contribution (v phr)	scientific (adj) ⊙
device (n) ⊙	make a decision (v phr)	technology (n) ⊙
diagram (n) ⊙	make a difference (v phr)	user (n) ⊙

⊙ = high-frequency words in the Cambridge Academic Corpus

	IN THIS UNIT YOU WILL ...
Watch and listen	watch and understand a video about College of Art graduate Christopher Raeburn.
Listening skills	take notes on main ideas and detail; identify auxiliary verbs for emphasis.
Critical thinking	create a purpose statement; evaluate interview questions.
Grammar	make predictions and talk about expectations for the future.
Speaking skills	ask for opinions and check information; ask follow-up questions.
Speaking task	take part in an interview to find out attitudes about uniforms and dress codes.

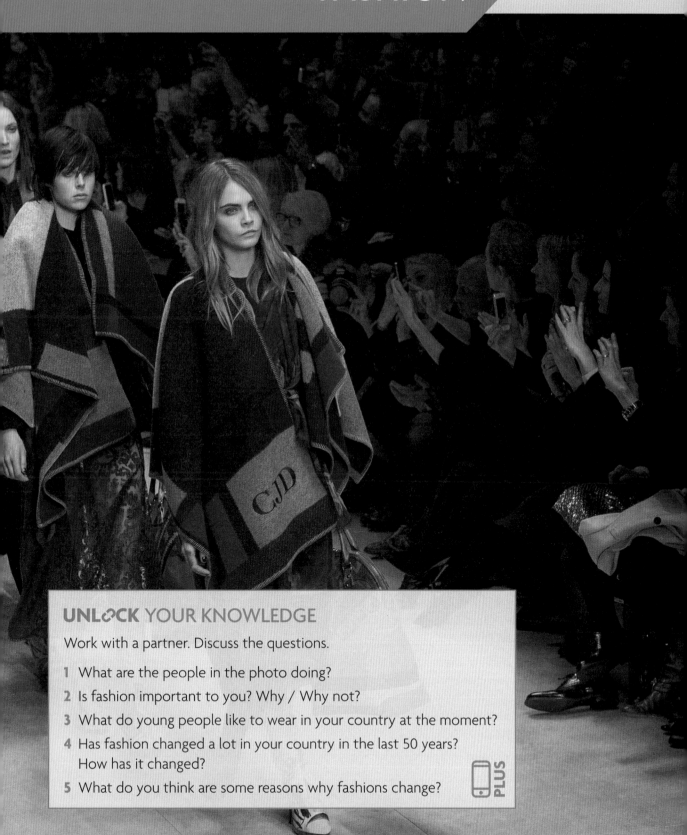

UNL⊘CK YOUR KNOWLEDGE

Work with a partner. Discuss the questions.

1 What are the people in the photo doing?
2 Is fashion important to you? Why / Why not?
3 What do young people like to wear in your country at the moment?
4 Has fashion changed a lot in your country in the last 50 years? How has it changed?
5 What do you think are some reasons why fashions change?

PLUS

WATCH AND LISTEN

PREPARING TO WATCH

ACTIVATING YOUR KNOWLEDGE

1 Work with a partner. Read the definitions in the box and discuss the questions below.

> **ethical brand** (n phr) a product which is produced in a way that does not hurt anyone or anything, for example, without hurting animals or underpaying workers
>
> **sustainable brand** (n phr) a product which is produced in a way that does not damage the environment

1 What ethical brands of clothing, furniture, etc. do you know of? What are the advantages of buying ethical brands? Are there any disadvantages?

2 What sustainable brands of food, clothing, etc. do you know of? What are the advantages of buying sustainable brands? Are there any disadvantages?

PREDICTING CONTENT USING VISUALS

2 You are going to watch a video about an ethical and sustainable fashion brand. Before you watch, look at the pictures. Circle the ideas you think you will hear.

1 The brand is from *England* / *the US* / *China*.
2 They make their clothes in *England* / *the US* / *China*.
3 They make the clothes with *new* / *special* / *recycled* materials.

GLOSSARY

military (adj) relating to the army

parachute (n) a large piece of material that is fixed to your body by strings and helps you to drop safely from an aircraft

production (n) all the things that you do in order to make a product which you then sell

fabric (n) cloth, material

garment (n) a piece of clothing

WHILE WATCHING

3 ▶ Watch the video and check your ideas in Exercise 2. Then, complete the sentence.

UNDERSTANDING MAIN IDEAS

Christopher Raeburn's fashions are sustainable and ethical because _____
_____ .

4 ▶ Watch again. Write *T* (true) or *F* (false) next to the statements. Correct the false statements.

UNDERSTANDING DETAIL

_____ 1 Christopher Raeburn started recycling military uniforms at university.

_____ 2 Christopher only uses old military uniforms to make his clothes.

_____ 3 Christopher employs people all over the world to make his clothes.

_____ 4 Some of Christopher's clothes are made from British wool.

_____ 5 At London Fashion Week, Christopher is showing his fashions in an old underground station.

_____ 6 Christopher has never worked with models at London Fashion Week before.

_____ 7 Christopher gets the ideas for his designs from nature.

5 ▶ Match the words in bold to their meaning. Circle either *a* or *b*. Watch again and check your ideas.

WORKING OUT MEANING FROM CONTEXT

1 I'm **based** here in London in the East End, Hackney Wick ...
   a from   b living and working

2 I never really **set out** to create an ethical or sustainable brand.
   a planned   b wanted

3 This season we're actually **splitting** the collection into three sections.
   a dividing   b choosing

4 That's very much focused on **incredibly** good quality ... wools.
   a definitely   b extremely

5 ... we'll be getting in and doing a very different event, it'll be **multimedia**.
   a many journalists will   b using film, pictures, music,
     come there   words, etc. together.

6 The ideas for Christopher's designs come firstly from the **original** fabric or piece of clothing ...
   a the first or earliest form   b the newest thing that
     of something   has been made

DISCUSSION

6 Work in small groups. Discuss the questions.

1 Why do you think Christopher Raeburn has been so successful?

2 What do you think of the designs you saw in the video?

3 Do you care about where the clothes you wear are made? Why / Why not?

4 Would you like to wear clothes made from sustainable fabrics? Why / Why not?

LISTENING

PREPARING TO LISTEN

UNDERSTANDING KEY VOCABULARY

1 You are going to listen to a discussion about clothes of the future. Before you listen, read the definitions. Complete the sentences with the words in bold.

> **convert** (v) to change something into something else
> **design** (n) the way in which something is arranged or shaped
> **fabric** (n) cloth, material
> **focus on** (phr v) to give a lot of attention to one subject or thing
> **local** (adj) relating to an area nearby
> **practical** (adj) suitable for the situation in which something is used
> **smart** (adj) operated by computer or digital technology
> **useless** (adj) not useful

1 Our clothes are made from 100% natural _____ .
2 My _____ shopping centre has lots of great clothing shops.
3 You don't need to pack boots. We're going on a beach holiday – they'll be _____ !
4 Solar panels _____ sunlight into energy.
5 _____ technology, like smartphones and smart watches, allows us to be constantly connected to the internet.
6 Those high-heeled shoes are not _____ for hiking up a mountain!
7 We're going to _____ clothes manufacturing, rather than fashion in general.
8 I love this shirt! The _____ is great.

PREDICTING CONTENT USING VISUALS

2 Work in small groups. Look at the photos. What topics do you think the discussion will focus on? Make a list of possible topics.

_____

_____

WHILE LISTENING

Taking notes on main ideas and details

Using an outline is an effective way to take notes while you listen. An outline helps you organize main ideas and details in a way that is easy to review later.

An outline is often organized like this:

I Topic

    A Main idea 1   **B** Main idea 2

       1 Detail 1   **1** Detail 1

       2 Detail 2   **2** Detail 2

       3 Detail 3   **3** Detail 3

3 🔊 7.1 Listen to the discussion and complete the outline.

TAKING NOTES ON
MAIN IDEAS

I Fashion of the (1)_____

   A Eco-clothes

   good for the (2)_____

   (3)_____ friendly

   not made by people working in bad (4)_____

   collect (5)_____ when you move

   energy converted into (6)_____

   B (7)_____ fabrics

   can (8)_____ bacteria

   can regulate body (9)_____

   can make (10)_____ clothing to help people

   exercise in hot or cold climates

   can reduce muscle aches and prevent us from getting

   (11)_____

   C Designers used (12)_____ in clothes

   (13)_____ made from lights

   change (14)_____ as you move

4 🔊 7.1 Listen to the discussion again. Write the adjective(s) the students use to describe each type of future clothing and whether their opinions are *P* (positive) or *N* (negative).

type of clothing	adjective(s)	speaker's opinion (*P* = positive, *N* = negative)
eco-clothes		
fabrics which regulate body temperature		
fabrics which prevent people from getting ill		
dress made of lights	(not very)	

POST-LISTENING

SKILLS

> ### Auxiliary verbs for emphasis
>
> In fluent speech, speakers usually contract auxiliary verbs (*am* → *'m*, *have* → *'ve*, etc.). However, to emphasize a point, they sometimes use the full form and stress the auxiliary verb.
>
> *That's interesting.*
> *That **is** interesting.* (= emphasizes that *that* is interesting)
>
> Speakers sometimes add *do* or *does* to an affirmative sentence to emphasize a point.
>
> *I like it.*
> *I **do** like it.* (= emphasizes that I like something or suggests that the listener didn't expect me to like it.)

5 🔊 7.2 Listen to the sentence pairs below. Underline the stressed word in each sentence.

1 a I've been reading about fashion of the future.
  b I have been reading about fashion of the future.
2 a That's amazing.
  b That is amazing.
3 a I agree that it's not very practical.
  b I do agree that it's not very practical.
4 a I think it'll be interesting.
  b I do think it'll be interesting.

6 Change the sentences to emphasize the verbs in bold by adding *do* or *does*.

1 I **believe** they can be used to make sports clothing.

_____

2 It **seems** we have a lot of ideas for the future of fashion.

_____

3 I **agree**.

_____

4 I **like** the idea of clothes which help people with health problems.

_____

5 She **buys** a lot of clothes.

_____

PRONUNCIATION FOR LISTENING

Vowel omission

Speakers don't always pronounce every letter in a word. Unstressed vowels are sometimes not pronounced when they appear between a consonant and /l/ or /r/.

Every is usually pronounced /ˈev·ri/.
Family is often pronounced /ˈfæm·li/.

Common words in which a vowel is often omitted

typically	favourite	different
jewellery	average	camera
basically	separate (adj)	temperature
finally	several	natural
chocolate	interesting	general

7 🔊 7.3 Listen to the extracts. For the words in bold, draw a line through the vowels which are not pronounced.

1 I've been looking for an **interesting** topic, but to be honest, I haven't come up with anything yet.
2 And eco-friendly clothing **typically** helps protect the environment, too.
3 Well, these fabrics keep your body **temperature** the same in any kind of weather.
4 Anyway, it looks like we've **finally** come up with some good ideas.
5 There are a lot of **different** articles on the topic.

8 🔊 7.3 Listen to the extracts again. Practise saying the sentences in Exercise 7.

DISCUSSION

9 Work with a partner. Discuss the questions.

1 What is your favourite item of clothing? Why?
2 Do you usually buy the latest fashion? Why / Why not?
3 Why do some people feel it's important to be fashionable?

⊙ LANGUAGE DEVELOPMENT

IDIOMS

Idioms are expressions which are often used in spoken English. An idiom doesn't always have a meaning which can easily be understood from looking at its individual words. You need to look at the whole expression to understand it.
I **keep my eye on** the fashion trends in other countries.
(= *watch something*)
Try to memorize any new idioms and use them when you speak.

1 Complete the sentences with the idioms from the box.

> are up for   give me a hand   go for it   I'm not a fan of
> keep my eye on   not really into   over the top

1 I've been looking for an interesting topic, but to be honest, I haven't come up with anything yet. Can you _____ ?
2 I'm _____ fashion …
3 I don't think many people _____ wearing a dress made of lights.
4 _____ that idea, to be honest.
5 It's pretty _____ ! As far as I'm concerned, a dress made from lights is useless.
6 I _____ the fashion trends in other countries.
7 Well, I hope you decide to _____ ! That would make a lot of women around the world very happy.

2 Match the idioms (1–7) in Exercise 1 to the meanings (a–g) below.
a to watch something __6__
b to make a big effort in order to achieve a goal _____
c to be not very interested in _____
d to want to do something _____
e help me _____
f to not like _____
g too extreme _____

PREDICTIONS AND EXPECTATIONS ABOUT THE FUTURE

GRAMMAR

There are several ways to make predictions or talk about your expectations for the future.

be going to

It's about future fabrics and how we**'re going to use** them. (expectation)

will

In the future, we**'ll** probably **wear** clothes which can regulate body temperature. (prediction)

Future continuous

The future continuous describes an action which will be in progress at a specific time in the future. Form the future continuous with *will* or *be going to* + *be* + verb + *-ing*.

So, a few years from now, we**'ll** probably **be using** this fabric to charge our phones, right?

In the future, we**'re going to be wearing** clothes which regulate our temperature.

In my opinion, people **won't be wearing** clothes with smart technology in the near future.

3 Complete the sentences with the future continuous form of the verbs in brackets.

1 Now 3D printers can print clothes. In a few years, maybe people _____ (print) most of their clothes instead of shopping for them.

2 I think that in 25 years, we _____ (wear) clothes which keep us healthy. We'll never get ill!

3 Ten years from now, people probably _____ (not use) laptops, tablets or phones. We _____ (do) all our computing with wearable technology.

4 My friend Adam is the CEO of a successful company which develops eco-clothes. In a few years, it's likely that he _____ (make) millions of dollars. I expect he _____ (live) in a mansion!

PLUS

4 Complete the sentences to make predictions about the future. Use each future form (*will*, *be going to*, future continuous) at least once. You can write about the topics in the box, or other topics.

> cars   communication   fashion   homes   science
> space travel   technology   the environment   your life

1 Ten years from now, _____
_____

2 By the time I'm 80, _____
_____

3 A hundred years from now, _____
_____

4 In the year 3000, _____
_____

5 Work with a partner. Share your answers to Exercise 4 and ask follow-up questions.

LISTENING 2

PREPARING TO LISTEN

UNDERSTANDING KEY VOCABULARY

1 You are going to listen to a radio interview. Before you listen, read the sentences (1–5) below and write the correct form of the words in bold next to the definitions (a–h).

1 Aysha's **collection** was presented during the last Fashion Week in Doha.
2 I have always tried to **combine** my culture with fashion.
3 As a teenager, I would make my own skirts and scarves. I wanted my designs to be **individual**. They were **unique** and, eventually, people **admired** my clothes rather than laughed at me.
4 Many traditional clothing **styles** are being reused by young designers.
5 My philosophy is to create clothes which are **modest** but, at the same time, give women **confidence**.

a _____ (v) to respect or approve of something
b _____ (adj) not showing too much of a person's body
c _____ (adj) different from everyone or everything else
d _____ (n) a selection of clothing designs which are sold at particular times of the year
e _____ (adj) considered as one thing, not part of a group
f _____ (v) to mix or join things together
g _____ (n) a feeling of being certain about yourself and your abilities
h _____ (n) a way of designing hair, clothes, furniture, etc.

PLUS

2 Work with a partner. Discuss the questions.

USING YOUR
KNOWLEDGE

1 What does the word *fashion* mean to you? Can you define it in ten words or fewer?
2 Does fashion allow people to show their personality or does it make people look and act the same?
3 Do you like the clothes in the photo? Why / Why not?

WHILE LISTENING

3 🔊 7.4 Listen to the first part of the interview. Answer the questions.

LISTENING FOR
MAIN IDEAS

1 Who is Aysha Al-Husaini? _____
2 Where was she born? _____
3 What is she famous for? _____

4 🔊 7.5 Listen to the second part of the interview and complete the outline.
Listen for the interviewer's questions to help identify the main ideas.

Interview with Aysha Al-Husaini

A Feelings about (1)_____

(2)_____

(3)_____

made own clothes - colourful skirts, scarves, etc.

B Misunderstandings about (4)_____

(5)_____

(6)_____

(7)_____

C Aysha's fashion
modest clothes which give women confidence

(8)_____

(9)_____

people like to be individuals, show their cultural roots

(10)_____

5 🔊 7.6 Listen to the interview again. Write T (true), F (false) or DNS (does
not say) next to the statements. Correct the false statements.

_____ 1 Aysha grew up in Doha.

_____

_____ 2 It can be difficult to buy long-sleeved clothes in New York.

_____

_____ 3 Aysha started making clothes when she was a teenager.

_____

_____ 4 Most Muslim women wear a *burka*.

_____

_____ 5 Aysha's teachers asked her why she didn't design Western styles
of clothing.

_____

_____ 6 Aysha's designs are for women who like to dress in a modest way.

_____

_____ 7 Many Muslim women want to wear fashionable clothes.

_____

_____ 8 Chinese and Indian designers don't use traditional designs.

_____

_____ 9 You can buy Aysha's collection in Malaysia and Singapore.

_____

POST-LISTENING

6 Look at your notes from the interview and answer the questions. Give reasons for your answers.

1 Is Aysha's work popular in the fashion world?

_____

_____

2 Did Aysha have problems growing up in New York?

_____

_____

3 Do some non-Muslim people understand what Muslim fashion is?

_____

_____

4 Was becoming a fashion designer easy for Aysha?

_____

_____

5 Is Aysha's fashion company successful?

_____

_____

DISCUSSION

7 Work in small groups. Use ideas from Listening 1 and Listening 2 to answer the following questions.

1 What are some of the different purposes of clothing design and fashion? Think about, for example, eco-clothes or Aysha Al-Husaini's work.

2 Do you think it's possible to combine fashion with tradition? Why / Why not?

3 Aysha says that her clothes 'give women confidence'. Do you agree that clothes can influence how people feel about themselves? Why / Why not?

4 Do you think it's better to dress in an individual way or to dress in a similar way to everyone else? Why?

SPEAKING

CRITICAL THINKING

At the end of this unit, you will do the speaking task below.

▶ Take part in an interview to find out attitudes about uniforms and dress codes.

SKILLS

Creating a purpose statement

Before interviewing someone, it is helpful to create a purpose statement – that is, a sentence about what you want to learn from the interview. A good purpose statement:
- is just one sentence.
- states the goal of the interview.
- uses qualitative words (*explore*, *understand*, *discover*, *learn about*).

The purpose of the interview is to learn how fashions have changed in the last five years and to explore fashion trends of the next decade.

 ANALYZE

1 Look at your outline from Listening 2 on page 158. Then, tick the best purpose statement for the interview with Aysha Al-Husaini in the list below. Why do you think it is best? What is wrong with the other statements?

   1 The purpose of the interview is to explore fashions from around the world. ☐

   2 The purpose of the interview is to find out about Aysha Al-Husaini's background and why she got into fashion design. In addition, I plan to learn about Muslim fashion and about Aysha's plans for her business. ☐

   3 The purpose of the interview is to learn about Aysha Al-Husaini's career as a fashion designer and her chic yet traditional Muslim fashions. ☐

2 Work in small groups. Discuss the questions. Reflect on your own experiences.

   1 What is a dress code?
   2 Why do some schools, universities and companies have a dress code?

 APPLY

3 Look at the speaking task. Write a purpose statement for your interview.

   My purpose statement: _____

   _____

Evaluating interview questions

In order to get interesting and relevant information from an interview, you need to ask good questions.

Good interview questions have these characteristics:

1 **They are open.** *Open questions* allow many possible answers. *Closed questions* limit the possible answers.

   Closed questions:

   Do you prefer the fashions of a decade ago or of today?
   (Answer choices: *a decade ago / today*)
   Are you interested in fashion? (Answer choices: *yes / no*)

   Open questions:

   What decade do you think had the most interesting fashions?
   How did you become interested in fashion?

2 **They are not biased.** Biased questions encourage the interviewee to answer in a certain way.

   Biased question: Don't you think fashions have become less attractive in the last five years? (Encourages a *yes* answer)

   Unbiased question: What's your opinion of how fashion has changed in the last five years? (Doesn't encourage a particular answer)

3 **They only have one part.** Two-part questions can confuse the interviewee. After they answer the first part, they might forget what the second part was.

   Two-part question: What is your opinion of how fashions have changed in the past five years and what do you think of today's fashions?

   One-part question: What do you think of today's fashions?

4 **They are focused.** Focused questions make it clear what type of answer you're looking for.

   Unfocused question: What do you think about the future? (It's not clear what aspect of the future you want to know about.)

   Focused question: What do you think fashions will be like in the future?

5 **They relate to your purpose.**

   Purpose: The purpose of the interview is to explore the future of fashion.

   Unrelated question: Who is your favourite fashion designer? (This doesn't relate to the future of fashion.)

   Related question: How do you think fashion will change in the next ten years?

ANALYZE

4 Read the purpose statement and the interview questions. What is wrong with each question? Match the problems (a–e) to the questions (1–5).

Purpose statement: The purpose of the interview is to learn about the fashions of the 1950s.

1 How did you become interested in 1950s fashion and when did you start researching it? _____
2 Do you like 1950s fashions? _____
3 What do you think of the films from the 1950s? _____
4 What do you think of fashion? _____
5 Don't you think that the fashions of the 1950s were boring? _____

a closed
b biased
c two-part
d unfocused
e doesn't relate to the purpose

APPLY

5 Work in small groups. Try to make a list of ten questions for your interview.

1 _____
2 _____
3 _____
4 _____
5 _____
6 _____
7 _____
8 _____
9 _____
10 _____

EVALUATE

6 Look at your questions in Exercise 5. Which are the best? Are there any which could be combined? Are there any which are not very interesting? In the same group, identify the five specific questions you would like to ask in your interview.

1 _____
2 _____
3 _____
4 _____
5 _____

PREPARATION FOR SPEAKING

ASKING FOR OPINIONS AND CHECKING INFORMATION

To ask someone for their opinion, you can use expressions like *Do you think that*, *Would you say that* and *Do you feel that* to introduce your questions.

Do most people know much about Muslim clothes? (= direct question)

Do you feel that / Would you say that / Do you think that most people know much about Muslim clothes? (= indirect question)

When you ask someone for their opinion, you can add phrases like *Can you tell me* and *Could you tell me* before questions to make them more indirect and polite.

How do you feel about Muslim fashion? (= direct question)

Can you tell me how you feel about Muslim fashion? (= indirect question)

To check that you understood something correctly, you can use the following phrases:

So, **are you saying that** there is a need for fashionable clothes for Muslim women?

Do you mean that Muslim women sometimes have a hard time finding fashionable clothes?

1 Circle the phrase which correctly completes each question.

1 *Can you tell me / Are you saying that* it's important to educate people about Muslim fashion?

2 *Do you mean that / How do you feel about* the idea of opening shops in Singapore and Malaysia?

3 *Would you say that / Could you tell me* many women are looking for modest clothes?

4 *Are you saying that / Can you tell me* how you feel about Muslim fashion?

2 Replace each direct question with an indirect question to make it more polite or to check information.

A: *What is the best way to dress for a job interview?*

(1)_____ ?

B: I think you should wear a suit and a tie.

A: *Should I wear a suit even if I don't usually wear one?*

(2)_____ ?

B: Yes, absolutely. As I see it, you only have 30 minutes to impress your future boss at the interview. You should look your best.

A: I'm not sure I agree. *Are my skills less important than what I look like?*

(3)_____ ?

B: No, I'm just saying that you should dress appropriately. *Are you really going to wear jeans and a T-shirt to your job interview?*

(4)_____ ?

A: I think so. The company I want to work for isn't interested in appearances.

ASKING FOLLOW-UP QUESTIONS

Asking follow-up questions is a useful interviewing strategy. If a person you are interviewing says something which you find interesting and you want to know more, you can ask follow-up questions to get more information about the topic.

To ask follow-up questions, use phrases like:

Can you explain why you decided to design fashions for Muslim women?

Why do you think that there is so much misunderstanding about Muslim clothes?

What do you mean by 'traditional chic'?

You mentioned that when you were a teenager, your friends thought you dressed strangely in the summer. **How did you feel about that?**

Could you expand on that point?

Can you tell me more about your plans to open shops in other cities?

3 For each statement, write a good follow-up question. Use phrases from the box above. Try not to use the same phrase more than once.

1 I'm planning to change my individual fashion style.
   Follow-up question: _____?

2 When I was in school, I used to hate my uniform.
   Follow-up question: _____?

3 My best friend Ellie has started to dress too young for her age.
   Follow-up question: _____?

4 A lot of people have strong feelings about dress codes at work.
   Follow-up question: _____?

5 Research has shown that students behave better in school when they wear uniforms.
   Follow-up question: _____?

4 Work in small groups. Share your questions in Exercise 3. For each statement, whose question do you think is the best? Why?

5 Look at the topics below. What is your opinion about them? Make notes about each of the topics.

- People should dress smartly for work every day.

  _____
  _____
  _____

- Secondary school students should wear uniforms to school.

  _____
  _____
  _____

- It's important to have an individual style and not to dress like everyone else.

  _____
  _____
  _____

- You should always look your best, even when you're just going out for coffee or to the supermarket.

  _____
  _____
  _____

6 Work in small groups. Share your opinions on the topics in Exercise 5. Ask the others in the group follow-up questions.

SPEAKING TASK

Take part in an interview to find out attitudes about uniforms and dress codes.

PREPARE

1 Look at the purpose statement and questions you created in Exercises 3 and 6 in the Critical thinking section. Review your notes.

2 Make your questions more polite. You can use language like this:

Can you tell me ...
Could you tell me ...
Do you think that ...

Would you say that ...
Do you feel that ...

3 Look at your questions from the the Critical thinking section. Are they in an order which makes sense? If not, change the order so it does make sense.

4 Refer to the Task checklist below as you prepare for your interview.

TASK CHECKLIST	✔
Ask questions in an order which makes sense.	
Ask for opinions politely and clearly.	
Check information where necessary.	
Ask follow-up questions.	

PRACTISE

5 Work with a partner. Practise your interview questions. Take notes on your partner's questions and how they could improve their interview.

6 Give each other feedback about your performance.

1 Were there enough questions? What other questions could you add?
2 Did the interviewer check information?
3 Did the student give clear opinions?

7 Make improvements to your questions based on your partner's feedback.

PRESENT

8 Work with a different partner. Interview your partner. Then, change roles and let your partner interview you.

OBJECTIVES REVIEW

1 Check your learning objectives for this unit. Write *3, 2* or *1* for each objective.

3 = very well   2 = well   1 = not so well

I can ...

watch and understand a video about College of Art graduate Christopher Raeburn.   _____

take notes on main ideas and detail.   _____

identify auxiliary verbs for emphasis.   _____

create a purpose statement.   _____

evaluate interview questions.   _____

make predictions and talk about expectations for the future.   _____

ask for opinions and check information.   _____

ask follow-up questions.   _____

take part in an interview to find out attitudes about uniforms and dress codes.   _____

2 Go to the *Unlock* Online Workbook for more practice with this unit's learning objectives.

WORDLIST

admire (v)	go for it (idiom)	over the top (idiom)
collection (n) ⊙	individual (adj) ⊙	practical (adj) ⊙
combine (v) ⊙	keep (one's) eye on (something) (idiom)	smart (adj)
confidence (n) ⊙		style (n) ⊙
convert (v) ⊙	local (adj) ⊙	unique (adj) ⊙
design (n) ⊙	modest (adj) ⊙	(be) up for (something) (idiom)
fabric (n) ⊙	not (be) a fan of (something) (idiom)	useless (adj)
focus on (phr v)		
give (someone) a hand (idiom)	(be) not really into (something) (idiom)	

⊙ = high-frequency words in the Cambridge Academic Corpus

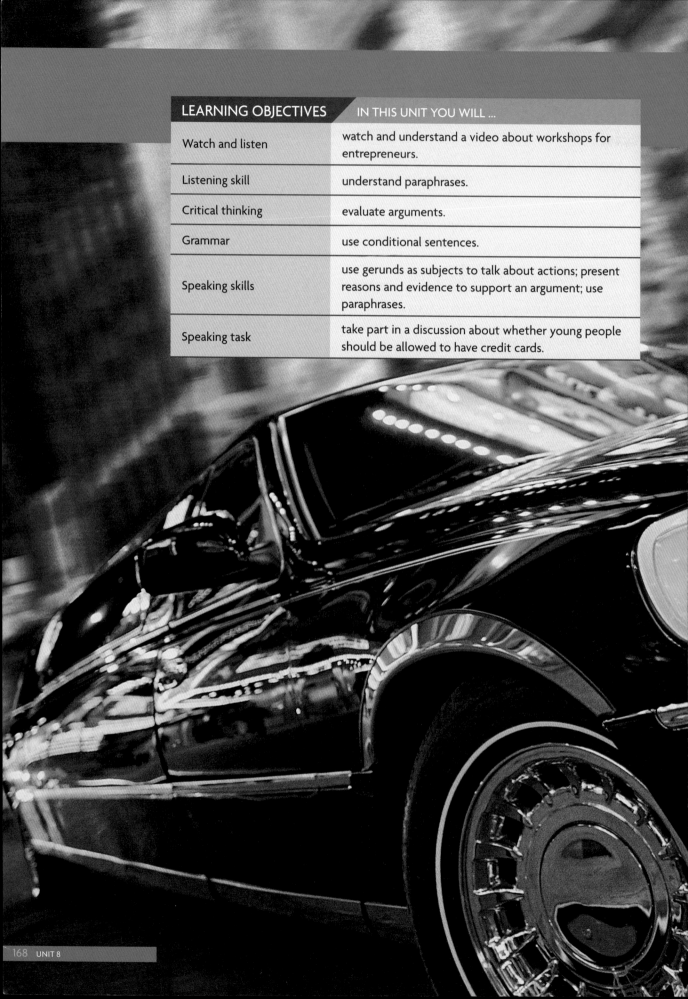

LEARNING OBJECTIVES

IN THIS UNIT YOU WILL ...

Watch and listen	watch and understand a video about workshops for entrepreneurs.
Listening skill	understand paraphrases.
Critical thinking	evaluate arguments.
Grammar	use conditional sentences.
Speaking skills	use gerunds as subjects to talk about actions; present reasons and evidence to support an argument; use paraphrases.
Speaking task	take part in a discussion about whether young people should be allowed to have credit cards.

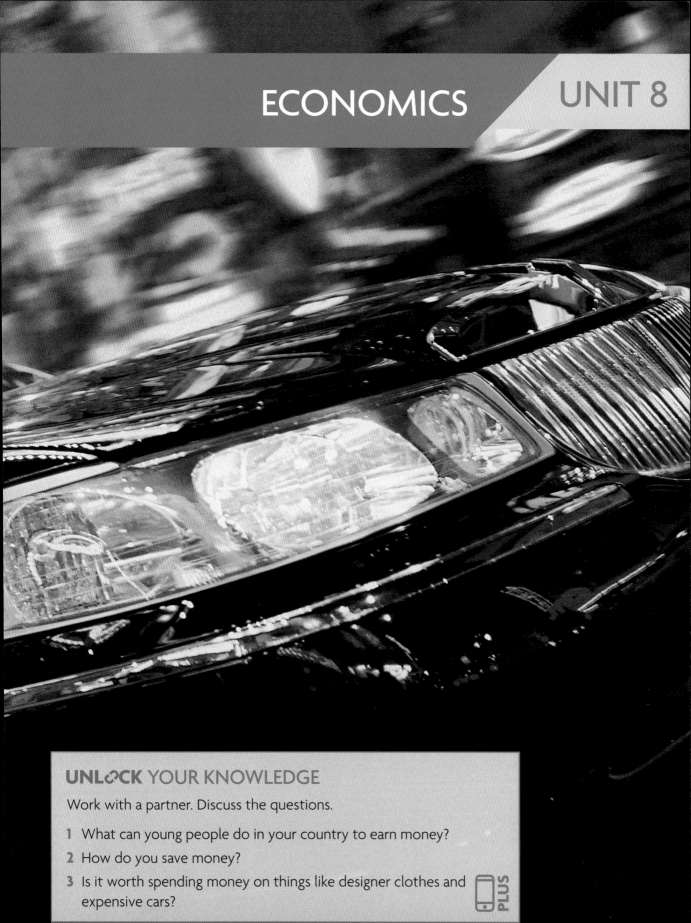

ECONOMICS

UNIT 8

UNL⬤CK YOUR KNOWLEDGE

Work with a partner. Discuss the questions.

1 What can young people do in your country to earn money?

2 How do you save money?

3 Is it worth spending money on things like designer clothes and expensive cars?

PREPARING TO WATCH

ACTIVATING YOUR KNOWLEDGE

1 Work with a partner. Discuss the questions.

   1 What companies were started by one or two people?
   2 Do you think most people need a lot of money to start a business? Why / Why not?
   3 What types of expensive equipment might someone need to buy when they start a business?

PREDICTING CONTENT USING VISUALS

2 Work with a partner. Look at the photos from the video and discuss the questions.

   1 What do you think TechShop is?
   2 What kinds of things do you think people make with these machines?
   3 Do you think the man in the suit works for TechShop? What could his job be?

GLOSSARY

get laid off (phr v) to lose one's job, usually because there is no work for the person to do

prototype (n) the first model or example of something new which can be developed or copied in the future

entrepreneur (n) someone who starts a business, especially when this involves seeing a new opportunity

machinery (n) machines, often large ones in a factory

partnership (n) the joining of two people or organizations to work together to achieve something

expand (v) to increase in size or amount or to cause something to do this

WHILE WATCHING

3 ▶ Watch the video. Fill in the blanks to complete the sentences.

UNDERSTANDING
MAIN IDEAS

1 TechShop offers people access to expensive _____ .
2 The entrepreneurs create prototypes of _____ they hope to sell.
3 The woman is making products for _____ .
4 One man has designed a special _____ cover.
5 Another man has created a way to make _____ cooler.
6 TechShop is expanding to more _____ .

4 ▶ Watch again. Write *T* (true), *F* (false) or *DNS* (does not say) next to the statements. Then, correct the false statements.

UNDERSTANDING
DETAIL

_____ 1 TechShop attracts people who like to work for others.

_____

_____ 2 People usually work in small groups at TechShop.

_____

_____ 3 Most people at TechShop like to buy things.

_____

_____ 4 Some of the inventors are now selling their products on the street.

_____

_____ 5 One man has hired 30 people.

_____

_____ 6 The success of TechShop shows that many people with a lot of money have great ideas.

_____

DISCUSSION

5 Work in small groups. Discuss the questions. Then, compare your answers with another group.

1 What are three differences between working for a small company (1–50 people) and a large company (50+ people)?
2 Would you like to own your own business? Why / Why not?
3 If you started a business, what kind of business would it be? Explain your answer.

LISTENING

LISTENING 1

PREPARING TO LISTEN

1 You are going to listen to a podcast about millionaire lifestyles. Before you listen, circle the best definition for the word or phrase in bold.

1 If you want to **save money**, you could stop eating out in expensive restaurants.
   a to lose money quickly
   b to keep money to use in the future

2 I just paid my university tuition fees. That's why I can't **afford** to go out this weekend.
   a to want to do something because it is cheap
   b to have enough money to buy or do something

3 Sarah took out a big **loan** to buy her first house.
   a an amount of money which you borrow and have to pay back
   b an amount of money you earn for doing work

4 He used his credit card to go on holiday. Now he has a huge **debt**.
   a money which is used for spending on flights, hotels, etc.
   b money which is owed to someone else

5 My cousin is a **millionaire**. He has three houses and four cars and he goes on exotic holidays every year.
   a a person who has more than 1,000,000 dollars, pounds, etc.
   b a person who spends all the money they have in the bank

6 I borrowed money to buy my car. Every month I have to make a £300 **payment**.
   a money a bank charges for using a credit card
   b an amount of money paid

7 Marta puts 10% of every monthly salary into the bank. She already has £15,000 in **savings**.
   a money you keep, usually in a bank
   b money you spend every month

2 Work with a partner. Discuss the questions.

1 What kinds of cars do you think millionaires drive?
2 What kinds of houses do they live in?
3 What kinds of clothes do they wear?

3 🔊 8.1 Look at the book cover and listen to the introduction to a podcast about millionaire lifestyles. Discuss the questions.

1 The speaker says that the results of the study were surprising. Can you guess why they were surprising?
2 What does *wealthy* mean?
3 What do you think the rest of the podcast will be about?

WHILE LISTENING

4 Work in small groups. Tick the behaviours of millionaires which you think are true.

LISTENING FOR
MAIN IDEAS

Millionaires ...
1 ☐ drive luxury cars and eat in expensive restaurants.
2 ☐ know how much money they spend on food, clothes, etc.
3 ☐ live in the same place for a long time.
4 ☐ don't spend a lot of money on cars.
5 ☐ have successful relationships.
6 ☐ borrow money from the bank.
7 ☐ are happy with what they have.
8 ☐ buy expensive things to feel better.

5 🔊 8.2 Listen to the podcast and underline the behaviours in Exercise 4 which it says are true of millionaires.

6 🔊 8.2 Listen to the podcast again. Complete the notes with numbers and percentages.

TAKING NOTES
ON DETAIL

Around (1)_____ % of millionaires know how much they spend every year.

(2)_____ % of millionaires have lived in the same house for (3)_____ years.

About (4)_____ % of millionaires live in homes which cost around the national (5)_____.

(6)_____ % of luxury cars are owned by people who can't afford them.

Understanding paraphrases

To help listeners understand what they're saying, speakers sometimes paraphrase. That is, they explain an idea in different words, often in a simpler or shorter way. To recognize paraphrases, listen for the phrases in bold, which often introduce paraphrases.

Most people think that rich people live <u>lavish lifestyles</u> – **that is**, they <u>drive very expensive cars, eat in expensive restaurants, own a yacht or live in big houses</u>.

Millionaires are often <u>financially savvy</u>. **To put it another way**, they're <u>smart about how to save and spend money</u>.

Most millionaires actually seem to have <u>ordinary lifestyles</u>. **In other words**, <u>they have normal cars, average houses and so on</u>.

Sometimes speakers paraphrase without using an introductory phrase.

John Holm decided to <u>study the behaviour of wealthy people</u>. He <u>paid close attention to what rich people do</u>.

7 Read the sentences. Underline the words or phrases in each sentence which mean the same thing.

1 The important lesson here is to live within your means – that is, don't spend more money than you have.

2 Instead, they have spent all their money trying to show off – showing other people that they might be wealthy.

3 Even though Liz is a millionaire, she's very frugal. In other words, she's careful about how she spends her money.

4 When I was growing up, my family was economically disadvantaged. To put it another way, we didn't have much money.

SKILLS

PRONUNCIATION FOR LISTENING

SKILLS

Silent letters

Some English words include letters which are not pronounced. This is because the pronunciation of the words has changed over time, but the spelling has stayed the same. For example, the letter *w* is not pronounced in *write* and the letter *b* is not pronounced in *comb*. There aren't any rules about which letters are silent and which are not. These words need to be learned individually.

8 🔊 8.3 Listen to the sentences. Pay attention to the pronunciation of the words in bold. Circle the letters which are not pronounced.

1 Most people think that rich people live lavish lifestyles, that is they drive very expensive cars, eat in expensive restaurants, own a **yacht** or live in big houses.

2 In other words, having expensive things is not always a **sign** that someone is rich.

3 On the other hand, people who look rich – the people who drive the latest Ferrari or only wear **designer** clothes – may not actually be rich at all.

4 As a result, they don't spend too much and they don't get into **debt**.

5 There is no **doubt** that it's more difficult to save money if you are single.

6 So, what can we learn from the wealthy? The **answer** is surprisingly simple.

9 Work with a partner. Take turns saying the sentences in Exercise 8.

DISCUSSION

10 Work alone. Decide if you agree with the points below from the podcast. Make notes to explain why / why not and think of examples from your own life.

1 Pay close attention to your money.
2 Don't spend more than you have.
3 Don't try to look rich.
4 Pay close attention to your relationships.
5 Be happy with what you have.

11 Work in small groups and share your ideas. Decide together which point you think is the most important and why.

⊙ LANGUAGE DEVELOPMENT

COLLOCATIONS WITH *PAY* AND *MONEY*

1 Read the definitions. Complete the sentences with the correct form of the words in bold.

> **borrow money** (v phr) to take money and promise to pay it back later
> **lose money** (v phr) to have less money than you had before
> **make money** (v phr) to earn money from a job or an investment
> **owe money** (v phr) to have to pay someone money you borrowed
> **pay a fine** (v phr) to pay money for not obeying a rule or law
> **pay in cash** (v phr) to pay for something with money (not a bank card)
> **pay off** (phr v) to pay the money that you owe
> **raise money** (v phr) to collect money from other people, often for charity
> **save money** (v phr) to keep money for use in the future
> **spend money** (v phr) to give money as a payment for something

1 My company didn't _____ last quarter. Our new products haven't been selling well.

2 I never use a credit card. I always _____ .

3 If you have a lot of debt, it's a good idea to _____ your loans a little bit every month.

4 Peter had to _____ for parking in an illegal place.

5 Investing in the stock market is risky. If you're not lucky, you might _____ .

6 My brother is going to _____ from my parents so he can buy a new car.

7 We want to _____ for our wedding, so we have to reduce our spending.

8 I _____ to my cousin. She lent me €20 for petrol last weekend.

9 The football team is trying to _____ to buy new shirts and shorts.

10 Maria isn't going on holiday with us because she doesn't want to _____ . She should get a job which pays more!

CONDITIONAL SENTENCES

GRAMMAR

Use *zero conditionals* to talk about general facts, truths and habits. Use *if* +
present simple in the *if*-clause. Use the present simple in the main clause.

      if + present simple

If people **have** a lot of money, they **are** happier.

                                  present simple

Use *first conditional* sentences to talk about things which are possible now or
in the future and their likely results. Use *if* + present simple in the *if*-clause and
a future verb form in the main clause.

      if + present simple

If we save a little money each month, we**'ll be able to** afford a holiday
in the summer.   future verb form

You can also use conditional sentences to give advice and suggestions. These
are formed with *if you ...* in the *if*-clause and an imperative in the main clause.

If you want to be rich, **save** a lot of money!

                      imperative

2 Look at the statements. Write *A* next to the sentences which give advice
  or make a suggestion and *T* next to the sentences which talk about things
  that are generally true or possible.

  1 If you want to be a millionaire, don't spend a lot on your house. _____

  2 If you don't have to worry about monthly credit card payments, you're
    less likely to buy things to make you feel better. _____

  3 If you change houses a lot and live in expensive places, it is impossible
    to save money. _____

  4 If you want to comment on these ideas, go to our website. _____

3 These sentences include mistakes. Delete, change or add one word in
  each sentence to make it correct.

  1 If you want to save money, you don't buy lots of expensive things.

    _____

  2 If you have time, listened to this podcast.

    _____

  3 If I have money, I always bought new clothes.

    _____

  4 If you will pay off all your debts, you will be happier.

    _____

  5 If I lose my job, I look for a new one.

    _____

4 Work with a partner. Match the sentence halves. Then, discuss the sentences. Which ones do you agree and disagree with? Why?

1 If I get a well-paid job, _____
2 If you want to be happy in the long term, _____
3 If I go to a restaurant, _____
4 If you spend more than you can afford, _____
5 If young people get credit cards, _____
6 If I can't afford to buy something, _____
7 If you plan your spending, _____
8 If I want to have a relaxing holiday, _____

a I always leave a big tip if the service is good.
b it is easier to save money.
c I always save up and buy it later.
d find a job you love.
e you will get into debt.
f they often spend too much money.
g I'll buy a house.
h I go to the beach.

5 Complete the sentences with your own ideas. Then, work with a partner and discuss your sentences. Give reasons for your answers. Ask each other follow-up questions.

1 If you want to save money, _____ .
2 If you want to be rich, _____ .
3 If you are careful with your money, _____ .
4 If you wear expensive clothes, _____ .
5 If you take nice holidays, _____ .
6 If you want to be happy, _____ .

6 Work in small groups. Think of ideas to complete the sentences below. Share your sentences with the other students. Respond to what they say with another conditional sentence.

If I get a better job, ...
If I stay up very late tonight, ...
If I learn to speak perfect English, ...

If I get a better job, I'll make a lot more money.

If you make a lot more money, you'll buy an expensive car.

If you buy an expensive car, you'll ...

PREPARING TO LISTEN

1 You are going to listen to a discussion about being paid for getting good grades in university. Before you listen, read the definitions. Complete the sentences with the correct form of the words in bold.

> **decision** (n) a choice which someone makes after thinking about the options
> **encourage** (v) to make someone more likely to do something
> **manage** (v) to control or organize something or someone
> **minimum wage** (n) the lowest pay for an hour's work which a worker can legally be paid
> **responsible** (adj) showing good judgement and able to be trusted
> **sense** (n) a quality of being or feeling loyal, responsible, etc.
> **services** (n) systems which supply things which people need

1 My teacher _____ me to apply to university. I followed her advice and I'm going to graduate next month!
2 Meg works at a restaurant for _____ . She doesn't make a lot of money, but it pays her rent.
3 She is a hardworking and _____ student. She always does her homework and gets to class on time.
4 I have trouble getting all of my work done on schedule. I need to learn to _____ my time better.
5 Because they need to make money, many young people make the _____ to work rather than go to university.
6 Going to university while working part-time requires a strong _____ of responsibility.
7 My school provides many _____ , including tutoring and career counselling.

2 🔊 8.4 Work in small groups. Listen to the introduction to the discussion and look at the question. What arguments do you think will be mentioned in the discussion? Complete the table with arguments for and against the idea.

> Should university students be paid for good grades?

for	against

WHILE LISTENING

3 🔊 8.5 Listen to the discussion. Write the arguments which the speakers mention in the table. Underline the arguments which were the same as your predictions.

for	against

4 🔊 8.6 Listen to part of the discussion again. Write the numbers you hear and what the numbers refer to.

	Numbers	What they refer to
1		
2		
3		
4		

POST-LISTENING

5 Look at the extracts from the discussion. Circle the correct answer to the question after each extract.

> I understand that many students drop out of university because of financial problems. ... However, will paying students really encourage them to continue?

1 The speaker thinks that ...
  a we should help students who have to leave university because they are poor.
  b paying students for good grades will not solve the problem.

> I can see your point, but we have already spent a lot on student services.

2 The speaker thinks ...
  a there is no point spending more on student services.
  b student services are a great way to solve the problem.

> I realize that students need encouragement to stay at university, but are we going in the right direction?

3 The speaker thinks paying students for good grades ...
  a will encourage them to stay at university.
  b might be a mistake.

6 Look again at the extracts in Exercise 5.

  1 Underline the phrases which are used to show that the speaker understands the other person's point of view.
  2 Circle the words which are used to show that the speaker is going to give a different point of view.

DISCUSSION

7 Work in small groups. Use ideas from Listening 1 and Listening 2 to answer the following questions.

  1 Which information in the listenings surprised you the most?
  2 Do you think students should be paid to go to university? What if they are the children of millionaires? Explain your answers.
  3 Do you think that being paid to get good grades would persuade a wealthy person to stay in university and work hard? Why / Why not?
  4 Do you think parents should pay their children for getting good grades? What are the advantages and disadvantages of doing this?

SPEAKING

CRITICAL THINKING

At the end of this unit, you will do the speaking task below.

> Take part in a discussion about whether young people should be allowed to have credit cards.

SKILLS

Evaluating arguments

When you think about a topic, it can be helpful to evaluate the various arguments and categorize them according to whether they are for or against a position. Then you can add supporting details.

1 Complete the table with arguments from Listening 2. Use information from your notes on page 181 and look at audio scripts 8.4 and 8.5 on pages 221–222.

UNDERSTAND

Position: University students should be paid for good grades.

arguments which support the position	arguments which oppose the position
Argument 1: Supporting details:	Argument 1: Supporting details:
Argument 2: Supporting details:	Argument 2: Supporting details:

2 Work with a partner. Read the news story and discuss the questions on page 184.

> With the financial difficulties faced by many countries around the world, more and more banks are reaching out to teenagers and university-age students. Many young people are sent advertisements for free credit cards as soon as they become old enough. As a result, many of them get into debt and start their adult lives owing money. This situation has started a public discussion about whether young people should be allowed to have credit cards.

1 Do you have a credit card? If yes, at what age did you get it?
2 If you don't have a credit card, would you like to have one? Why?
3 What are some of the problems with credit cards?
4 What is the best age to have your first credit card? Why?

EVALUATE

3 Work alone. Make a list of the advantages and disadvantages of allowing young people to have credit cards.

advantages

1 _____

2 _____

3 _____

4 _____

disadvantages

1 _____

2 _____

3 _____

4 _____

4 Work with a partner and discuss your ideas from Exercise 3.

APPLY

5 Work alone. Decide which side of the argument you support. Complete the table with your three best arguments and supporting details. Then, think of counter-arguments someone who supports the other side might use. How would you respond to these?

my position: _____	possible counter-arguments
Argument 1: Supporting details:	Counter-argument 1: Response:
Argument 2: Supporting details:	Counter-argument 2: Response:
Argument 3: Supporting details:	Counter-argument 3: Response:

USING GERUNDS AS SUBJECTS TO TALK ABOUT ACTIONS

> **LANGUAGE**
>
> The gerund is the *-ing* form of a verb. It functions as a noun and can act as the subject of a sentence.
>
> To focus on an action, use a gerund in a noun phrase at the start of a sentence. Make this noun phrase the subject of the sentence and put it before the main verb. The main verb is in the singular form.
>
> **Doing** small jobs for money **teaches** children how to be responsible.
>   gerund
>
> Make a sentence negative by adding *not* before the gerund.
>
> **Not teaching** children about money **is** a disadvantage in later life.
>   gerund

1 Underline the subject in the sentences.

  1 Learning should be about studying new things and improving yourself.
  2 Saving money is not easy if you have bills to pay.
  3 Reading books about millionaires is not a good way to get rich.
  4 Teaching children about money should start at an early age.

2 Rewrite the sentences to focus more on the actions in bold.

  1 It is not a good idea to **pay children for housework**.
    Paying children for housework is not a good idea.

  2 It is very important to **teach children to save money**.

  _____

  3 You can encourage children to study if you **pay them**.

  _____

  4 You can spoil children at an early age if you **give them money**.

  _____

  5 It's difficult to **learn about money** when you're a child.

  _____

  6 If you **don't have much money** it makes it difficult to start a family.

  _____

3 Work with a partner. Complete the sentences with your own ideas.

1 Teaching children about money is _____ .
2 Giving money to charity is _____ .
3 Being a millionaire is _____ .
4 Not saving money is _____ .
5 Spending money on luxury cars is _____ .
6 Buying designer clothes is _____ .

PRESENTING REASONS AND EVIDENCE TO SUPPORT AN ARGUMENT

SKILLS

Speakers use reasons and evidence to make their argument stronger and persuade listeners to agree with them. You can use these phrases to introduce reasons and evidence:

One effect/result/consequence of being a couple is that it's easier to save money. If there are two of you, it's easier to pay attention to how much money you have and what you're spending.

However, will paying students really encourage them to continue? **In my experience**, it won't.

Advisors can help students learn to manage their time better. **As a consequence / As a result / Because of that**, students will do better at university and will be more likely to graduate.

Because of / Due to the high cost of living, we had to move out of the city.

PLUS

4 Circle the correct phrase in each sentence.

1 Around 75% of millionaires know exactly how much money they have and they know exactly how much they spend on food, bills, clothes, etc. *As a result / In my experience*, they don't spend too much and they don't get into debt.

2 *One effect of / As a result of* paying university students would be that more students would finish their education.

3 *Due to / As a consequence* the huge sales of the app he designed, he became a millionaire almost overnight.

4 *One consequence of / In my experience,* treating students like adults makes them more responsible.

5 *As a consequence of / Because of that* saving money, they can plan for their future.

6 Millionaires often buy houses which aren't very expensive. *Because of that, / One consequence of* they are able to save a lot of money.

PLUS

USING PARAPHRASES

To make your arguments clearer, use paraphrases. Paraphrases can help you explain or summarize something you think your audience might not understand very well. Paraphrases also help your listeners remember the information by letting them hear it a second time.

The first important thing is that millionaires always have a good handle on their budget. **In other words**, they know how much they're spending. In John Holm's opinion, being 'wealthy' is a feeling. **That is**, it doesn't mean being rich or having millions. It means being happy with what you have.

They don't spend too much and they don't get into debt. They can plan for the future and save their money. **To sum up**, the lesson here is that you should never spend more money than you have!

5 Complete the paraphrases. Then, read your paraphrases to a partner. Did your partner understand what you were saying?

1 I can't afford to buy a new car right now. In other words, _____
_____ .

2 Millionaires often have simple lifestyles. That is, _____
_____ .

3 So, what can we learn from the wealthy? The answer is surprisingly simple. To sum up, _____ .

4 Students need encouragement to stay at university. To put it another way,
_____ .

5 We've talked a lot about the effects of paying students to attend university. To sum up, _____ .

6 When young adults have the choice between going to university or making money, they often make the wrong decision. That is,
_____ .

SPEAKING TASK

> Take part in a discussion about whether young people should be allowed to have credit cards.

PREPARE

1 Look at the table you created in Exercise 5 in the Critical thinking section. Review your notes and add any new information.

2 Refer to the Task checklist below as you prepare your points for the discussion.

TASK CHECKLIST	✔
Use collocations with *pay* and *money* correctly.	
Used conditional sentences correctly.	
Use gerunds to talk about actions clearly.	
Present reasons and evidence to support your argument.	
Use paraphrases.	

PRACTISE

3 Work in small groups. Discuss your opinions about whether young people should be allowed to have credit cards. Give your reasons and evidence.

4 Discuss the questions in your group.

1 Was your point of view strong and well-presented?

2 What could you improve about your arguments?

DISCUSS

5 Work in different groups. Each group should have some students who agree with the topic and some who disagree. Discuss the topic.

OBJECTIVES REVIEW

1 Check your learning objectives for this unit. Write *3, 2* or *1* for each objective.

3 = very well   2 = well   1 = not so well

I can ...

watch and understand a video about workshops for entrepreneurs.   _____

understand paraphrases.   _____

evaluate arguments.   _____

use conditional sentences.   _____

use gerunds as subjects to talk about actions.   _____

present reasons and evidence to support an argument.   _____

use paraphrases.   _____

take part in a discussion about whether young people should be allowed to have credit cards.   _____

2 Go to the *Unlock* Online Workbook for more practice with this unit's learning objectives.

UNLOCK ONLINE

WORDLIST		
afford (v) ⊙	manage (v) ⊙	raise money (v phr)
borrow money (v phr)	millionaire (n)	responsible (adj) ⊙
debt (n) ⊙	minimum wage (n)	save money (v phr)
decision (n) ⊙	owe money (v phr)	savings (n pl) ⊙
encourage (v) ⊙	pay a fine (v phr)	sense (n) ⊙
loan (n) ⊙	pay in cash (v phr)	service (n) ⊙
lose money (v phr)	pay off (phr v)	spend money (v phr)
make money (v phr)	payment (n) ⊙	

⊙ = high-frequency words in the Cambridge Academic Corpus

GLOSSARY

⊙ = high-frequency words in the Cambridge Academic Corpus

Vocabulary	Pronunciation	Part of speech	Definition
UNIT 1			
abandon ⊙	/əˈbændən/	(v)	to leave someone or something somewhere, sometimes not returning to get them
abuse ⊙	/əˈbjuːs/	(n)	violent or unfair treatment of someone
abuse ⊙	/əˈbjuːz/	(v)	to treat someone violently or unfairly
analyze ⊙	/ˈænəlaɪz/	(v)	to study or examine something in detail, in order to discover more about it
communicate ⊙	/kəˈmjuːnɪkeɪt/	(v)	to share information with others by speaking, writing, moving your body or using other signals
conditions ⊙	/kənˈdɪʃəns/	(n pl)	the situation in which someone lives or works
connect ⊙	/kəˈnekt/	(v)	to join two things or places together
cruel	/ˈkruːəl/	(adj)	not kind
damage ⊙	/ˈdæmɪdʒ/	(v)	to hurt
debate ⊙	/dɪˈbeɪt/	(v)	to discuss a subject in a formal way
depend on	/dɪˈpend ɒn/	(phr v)	to need
endangered	/ɪnˈdeɪndʒəd/	(adj)	at risk of no longer existing
environment ⊙	/ɪnˈvaɪərənmənt/	(n)	the air, land and water where people, animals and plants live
habitat ⊙	/ˈhæbɪtæt/	(n)	the natural environment of an animal or plant
involve ⊙	/ɪnˈvɒlv/	(v)	if a situation or activity involves something, that thing is a necessary part of it

Vocabulary	Pronunciation	Part of speech	Definition
issue ⊙	/'ɪʃuː/	(n)	a topic or problem which causes concern and discussion
melt	/melt/	(v)	to become liquid as a result of heating
protect ⊙	/prə'tekt/	(v)	to keep safe from danger
source ⊙	/sɔːs/	(n)	where something comes from
species ⊙	/'spiːʃiːz/	(n)	a group of plants or animals which share similar features
suffer ⊙	/'sʌfə/	(v)	to feel pain or unhappiness
support ⊙	/sə'pɔːt/	(v)	to agree with an idea, group or person
survive ⊙	/sə'vaɪv/	(v)	to continue to live, in spite of danger and difficulty
threat ⊙	/θret/	(n)	the possibility of trouble, danger or disaster
welfare	/'welfeə/	(n)	someone's or something's health and happiness

UNIT 2

Vocabulary	Pronunciation	Part of speech	Definition
affordable	/ə'fɔːdəbl/	(adj)	not expensive
alternative ⊙	/ɔːl'tɜːnətɪv/	(adj)	different from what is usual or traditional
benefit ⊙	/'benɪfɪt/	(n)	advantage
crisis ⊙	/'kraɪsɪs/	(n)	a very dangerous or difficult situation
disaster ⊙	/dɪ'zɑːstə/	(n)	a terrible accident which causes a lot of damage
environmental ⊙	/ɪnvaɪərən'mentəl/	(adj)	relating to the air, water and land
limited ⊙	/'lɪmɪtɪd/	(adj)	small in amount or number
long-term ⊙	/lɒŋ'tɜːm/	(adj)	continuing for a long time
opponent ⊙	/ə'pəʊnənt/	(n)	someone who disagrees with an idea

Vocabulary	Pronunciation	Part of speech	Definition
pollute	/pə'luːt/	(v)	to make something, like air or water, dirty or harmful
provide ⊙	/prə'vaɪd/	(v)	to give something
resource ⊙	/rɪ'zɔːs/	(n)	something you have and can use
risk ⊙	/rɪsk/	(n)	the possibility of something bad happening
solution ⊙	/sə'luːʃən/	(n)	a way of solving a problem
system ⊙	/'sɪstəm/	(n)	a way of doing things

UNIT 3

Vocabulary	Pronunciation	Part of speech	Definition
avoid ⊙	/ə'vɔɪd/	(v)	to stay away from something or not allow yourself to do something
break the law	/breɪk ðə lɔː/	(v phr)	to fail to obey the rules of a country, state or city
compare ⊙	/kəm'peə/	(v)	to look for the difference between two or more things
consist of	/kən'sɪst əv/	(phr v)	to be made of something
control ⊙	/kən'trəʊl/	(v)	to limit something
convenient ⊙	/kən'viːniənt/	(adj)	easy to use or suiting your plans well
crash	/kræʃ/	(n)	an accident in which a vehicle hits something
cure ⊙	/kjʊə/	(n)	something which will make an ill person healthy again
extreme ⊙	/ɪk'striːm/	(adj)	very severe or bad
figure out	/fɪgər 'aʊt/	(phr v)	to think about a problem until you know the answer
fine ⊙	/faɪn/	(n)	money which has to be paid as a punishment for not obeying a law
impact ⊙	/'ɪmpækt/	(n)	effect

Vocabulary	Pronunciation	Part of speech	Definition
influence ⊙	/'ɪnfluəns/	(v)	to affect how someone acts or thinks
injure	/'ɪndʒə/	(v)	to hurt or cause physical harm
method ⊙	/'meθəd/	(n)	a way of doing something
pass ⊙	/pɑːs/	(v)	to go past something or someone
prevent ⊙	/prɪ'vent/	(v)	to stop something from happening
respect ⊙	/rɪ'spekt/	(n)	polite behaviour towards someone
safety ⊙	/'seɪfti/	(n)	the condition of not being in danger
scared	/skeəd/	(adj)	feeling frightened or worried
serious ⊙	/'sɪəriəs/	(adj)	important; bad
solve ⊙	/sɒlv/	(v)	to find a way to fix a problem
trouble ⊙	/'trʌbl/	(n)	problems

UNIT 4

Vocabulary	Pronunciation	Part of speech	Definition
acceptable ⊙	/ək'septəbəl/	(adj)	satisfactory and able to be agreed to or approved of; good enough
agreement ⊙	/ə'griːmənt/	(n)	the situation in which people have the same opinion, or in which they approve of or accept something
anniversary	/ænɪ'vɜːsəri/	(n)	the day on which an important event happened in a previous year
behaviour ⊙	/bɪ'heɪvjər/	(n)	a particular way of acting
celebration	/selə'breɪʃən/	(n)	doing something to mark a special day or event
commercial ⊙	/kə'mɜːʃəl/	(adj)	relating to buying and selling things
die out	/daɪ aʊt/	(phr v)	to become rare and then disappear
event	/ɪ'vent/	(n)	anything which happens, especially something important or unusual
frighten	/'fraɪtən/	(v)	to make someone feel fear

Vocabulary	Pronunciation	Part of speech	Definition
generation	/dʒenə'reɪʃən/	(n)	all the people of about the same age within a society or a family
graduate	/'grædʒueɪt/	(v)	to complete university or college successfully
interact	/ɪntər'ækt/	(v)	to communicate and do things with someone or something
multicultural	/mʌlti'kʌltʃərəl/	(adj)	including people who have many different customs and beliefs
obligation ⊙	/ɒblɪ'geɪʃən/	(n)	something which you have to do
occasion ⊙	/ə'keɪʒən/	(n)	a special event or ceremony
personal ⊙	/'pɜːsənəl/	(adj)	relating to an individual person and not anyone else
political ⊙	/pə'lɪtɪkəl/	(adj)	relating to the activities of the government
social ⊙	/'səuʃəl/	(adj)	relating to a large group of people who live together in an organized way
specialize	/'speʃəlaɪz/	(v)	to spend most of your time studying one particular subject or doing one type of business
thoughtful	/'θɔːtfəl/	(adj)	showing care and consideration in how you treat other people

UNIT 5

Vocabulary	Pronunciation	Part of speech	Definition
come down with	/kʌm 'daʊn wɪð/	(phr v)	to get an illness, especially one which is not serious
concentration ⊙	/kɒnsən'treɪʃən/	(n)	the ability to give your whole attention to one thing
cultural ⊙	/'kʌltʃərəl/	(adj)	relating to the habits, traditions and beliefs of a society
cut down on	/kʌt 'daʊn ɒn/	(phr v)	to eat or drink less of something
educational ⊙	/edʒʊ'keɪʃənəl/	(adj)	relating to learning

Vocabulary	Pronunciation	Part of speech	Definition
emotional ⊙	/ɪ'məʊʃənəl/	(adj)	relating to feelings
get over	/get 'əʊvə/	(phr v)	to become healthy again after having an illness
give up	/gɪv 'ʌp/	(phr v)	to stop a habit, often because it is unhealthy
habit ⊙	/'hæbɪt/	(n)	something which you do regularly
illness ⊙	/'ɪlnəs/	(n)	a disease of the body or mind
intellectual ⊙	/ɪntəl'ektʃuəl/	(adj)	relating to your ability to think and understand things, especially complicated ideas
join in	/dʒɔɪn 'ɪn/	(phr v)	to agree to become involved in an organized activity
mental ⊙	/'mentəl/	(adj)	relating to the mind
overweight	/əʊvə'weɪt/	(adj)	being heavier than you want or than is good for you
participate ⊙	/pɑː'tɪsɪpeɪt/	(v)	to be involved in an activity
performance ⊙	/pə'fɔːməns/	(n)	how well a person does an activity
personal ⊙	/'pɜːsənəl/	(adj)	relating to a single person rather than to a group
physical ⊙	/'fɪzɪkəl/	(adj)	relating to the body
prove ⊙	/pruːv/	(v)	to show that something is true
reduce ⊙	/rɪ'djuːs/	(v)	to make (something) less in size, amount, etc.
relax	/rɪ'læks/	(v)	to become less tense or worried
sign up for	/saɪn 'ʌp fɔː/	(phr v)	to become involved in an activity with other people
social ⊙	/'səʊʃəl/	(adj)	relating to activities in which you meet and spend time with other people
stress	/stress/	(n)	worry caused by a difficult situation

Vocabulary	Pronunciation	Part of speech	Definition
take up	/teɪk ˈʌp/	(phr v)	to start doing a particular job or activity
treatment	/ˈtriːtmənt/	(n)	a way to cure an illness or injury
try out for	/traɪ ˈaʊt fɔː/	(phr v)	to compete for a position on a sports team or a part in a play
unhealthy	/ʌnˈhelθi/	(adj)	not good for your health; not strong and well
work out	/wɜːk ˈaʊt/	(phr v)	to exercise in order to make your body stronger

UNIT 6

Vocabulary	Pronunciation	Part of speech	Definition
access ☉	/ˈækses/	(v)	to be able to enter or use something
allow ☉	/əˈlaʊ/	(v)	to make it possible for someone to do something
app	/æp/	(n)	(abbreviation for *application*) software designed for a particular purpose which you can download onto a smartphone or other mobile device
create ☉	/kriˈeɪt/	(v)	to make something new or invent something
design ☉	/dɪˈzaɪn/	(v)	to make or draw plans for something
develop ☉	/dɪˈveləp/	(v)	to make something over a period of time
device ☉	/dɪˈvaɪs/	(n)	a piece of equipment which is used for a particular purpose
diagram ☉	/ˈdaɪəgræm/	(n)	a simple picture which shows how something works or what it looks like
discover ☉	/dɪˈskʌvə/	(v)	to find information, a place or an object, especially for the first time
industry ☉	/ˈɪndəstri/	(n)	the companies and activities involved in the process of producing goods for sale

Vocabulary	Pronunciation	Part of speech	Definition
install	/ɪnˈstɔːl/	(v)	to put new software onto a computer or mobile device
invent	/ɪnˈvent/	(v)	to create something which had never been made before
make a comparison	/meɪk ə kəmˈpærɪsən/	(v phr)	to consider the similarities between two things
make a contribution	/meɪk ə kɒntrɪˈbjuːʃən/	(v phr)	to help to make something successful
make a decision	/meɪk ə dɪˈsɪʒən/	(v phr)	to choose
make a difference	/meɪk ə ˈdɪfərəns/	(v phr)	to change something
make an investment	/meɪk ən ɪnˈvestmənt/	(v phr)	to put money into something to make a profit
make attempts	/meɪk əˈtempts/	(v phr)	to try
make improvements	/meɪk ɪmˈpruːvmənts/	(v phr)	to make something better
make public	/meɪk ˈpʌblɪk/	(v phr)	to share information about something
product ◉	/ˈprɒdʌkt/	(n)	something which is made to be sold
scientific ◉	/saɪənˈtɪfɪk/	(adj)	relating to the study of science
technology ◉	/tekˈnɒlədʒi/	(n)	knowledge, equipment and methods used in science and industry
user ◉	/ˈjuːzə/	(n)	someone who uses a product, machine or service

UNIT 7

admire	/ədˈmaɪə/	(v)	to respect or approve of something
collection ◉	/kəˈlekʃən/	(n)	a selection of clothing designs which are sold at particular times of the year
combine ◉	/kəmˈbaɪn/	(v)	to mix or join things together

Vocabulary	Pronunciation	Part of speech	Definition
confidence ⊙	/ˈkɒnfɪdəns/	(n)	a feeling of being certain about yourself and your abilities
convert ⊙	/kənˈvɜːt/	(v)	to change something into something else
design ⊙	/dɪˈzaɪn/	(n)	the way in which something is arranged or shaped
fabric ⊙	/ˈfæbrɪk/	(n)	cloth, material
focus on	/ˈfəʊkəs ɒn/	(phr v)	to give a lot of attention to one subject or thing
give (someone) a hand	/gɪv ə ˈhænd/	(idiom)	help (someone)
go for it	/ˈgəʊ fər ɪt/	(idiom)	to make a big effort in order to achieve a goal
individual ⊙	/ɪndɪˈvɪdʒuəl/	(adj)	considered as one thing, not part of a group
keep (one's) eye on (something)	/kiːp ˈaɪ ɒn/	(idiom)	to watch (something)
local ⊙	/ˈləʊkəl/	(adj)	relating to an area nearby
modest ⊙	/ˈmɒdɪst/	(adj)	not showing too much of a person's body
(be) not a fan of (something)	/nɒt ə ˈfæn əv/	(idiom)	to not like
(be) not really into (something)	/nɒt rɪəli ˈɪntu/	(idiom)	to be not very interested in
over the top	/əʊvə ðə ˈtɒp/	(idiom)	too extreme
practical ⊙	/ˈpræktɪkəl/	(adj)	suitable for the situation in which something is used
smart	/smɑːt/	(adj)	operated by computer or digital technology
style ⊙	/staɪl/	(n)	a way of designing hair, clothes, furniture, etc.

Vocabulary	Pronunciation	Part of speech	Definition
unique ⊙	/juː'niːk/	(adj)	different from everyone or everything else
(be) up for (something)	/ʌp fɔː/	(idiom)	to want to do (something)
useless	/'juːsləs/	(adj)	not useful
UNIT 8			
afford ⊙	/ə'fɔːd/	(v)	to have enough money to buy or do something
borrow money	/bɒrəʊ 'mʌni/	(v phr)	to take money and promise to pay it back later
debt ⊙	/det/	(n)	money which is owed to someone else
decision ⊙	/dɪ'sɪʒən/	(n)	a choice that someone makes after thinking about the options
encourage ⊙	/ɪn'kʌrɪdʒ/	(v)	to make someone more likely to do something
loan ⊙	/ləʊn/	(n)	an amount of money which you borrow and have to pay back
lose money	/luːz mʌni/	(v phr)	to have less money than you had before
make money	/meɪk mʌni/	(v phr)	to earn money
manage ⊙	/'mænɪdʒ/	(v)	to control or organize something or someone
millionaire	/mɪljə'neə/	(n)	a person who has more than one million dollars, pounds, etc.
minimum wage	/mɪnɪməm 'weɪdʒ/	(n)	the lowest pay for an hour's work which a worker can legally be paid
owe money	/əʊ mʌni/	(v phr)	to have to pay someone money which you borrowed
pay a fine	/peɪ ə faɪn/	(v phr)	to pay money as a punishment for not obeying a rule or law

Vocabulary	Pronunciation	Part of speech	Definition
pay in cash	/peɪ ɪn kæʃ/	(v phr)	to pay for something with money (not a credit card)
pay off	/peɪ ɒf/	(phr v)	to pay the money that you owe
payment ⊙	/ˈpeɪmənt/	(n)	an amount of money paid
raise money	/reɪz mʌni/	(v phr)	to collect money from other people, often for charity
responsible ⊙	/rɪˈspɒnsəbl/	(adj)	showing good judgement and able to be trusted
save money	/seɪv mʌni/	(v phr)	to keep money for use in the future
savings ⊙	/ˈseɪvɪŋz/	(n pl)	money you keep, usually in a bank
sense ⊙	/sens/	(n)	a quality of being or feeling loyal, responsible, etc.
service ⊙	/ˈsɜːvɪs/	(n)	a system which supplies things that people need
spend money	/spend mʌni/	(v phr)	to give money as a payment for something

VIDEO AND AUDIO SCRIPTS

UNIT 1

▶ The mental skills of chimpanzees

Narrator: For 30 years, scientists at Georgia State University have been studying the mental skills of chimpanzees. They're finding out if chimpanzees can plan ahead and how much they plan ahead.

Man: OK, I'm going to set up the computer, right here.

Narrator: They use a computer maze to find out about the chimpanzee's ability. In the wild, chimpanzees have to find food and protect themselves, so they probably need to make plans. But how good are they at planning?

One of the chimpanzees, named Panzee, is excellent. She can often complete difficult mazes that she's never seen before better than humans.

Man: Tell me what you want.

Narrator: This is an amazing discovery! Panzee doesn't make many mistakes and she can sometimes see the solution to the maze faster than a human can. The ability to look ahead and find the way from the beginning to the end of the maze means she's very smart.

And it means that planning before acting is not just a human skill.

Scientist: Chimpanzees do plan ahead. I don't believe that they can plan ahead nearly so far as we can. I think also that they reflect upon the past but not to the degree that we do. I would suggest that chimpanzees are able to plan ahead over the course of several days, whereas we can plan ahead for years or centuries if we wish.

 1.1

Host: Hello and welcome. Today's debate is on using animals for work. The first animal that was domesticated by humans is the dog. Even now, dogs are still used to **protect** our houses and keep us safe. Other domesticated animals – used for food – include sheep, cows and goats. The first donkeys were used by humans approximately 6,000 years ago in Egypt. Horses were domesticated 5,000 years ago in Europe and Asia. All these animals have been used to help human beings **survive**, either by providing food or by working for us. Horses, camels, elephants – they have all helped humans explore their land and transport goods from one place to another. But is this fair? What about animal rights? To argue for this **issue** today we have Amy Johnson, an animal rights activist and writer. To argue against the issue is Dr Jacob Kuryan. Dr Kuryan is a professor of zoology, which is the scientific study of animals, and a writer of several books on animal **welfare**. You both have two minutes to introduce your point of view. Ms Johnson, would you like to begin?

Ms Johnson: Thank you for inviting me to this debate. It's well known that animals have worked side by side with humans for thousands of years. In fact, they helped us develop our civilization and helped humans survive. Animals, like elephants and horses, were used to build amazing structures, like the pyramids in Egypt. Yet their hard work and suffering are hardly ever recognized. For example, horses, camels and elephants were used to transport armies and soldiers during wars and many of these animals died in these wars. And there are other examples. Even now, dogs are used to pull sleds in cold climates and elephants are used for logging. These animals work long hours and live in difficult **conditions**. However, they get very little reward. Humans just use them to their advantage. My main argument is that in the modern world, there is no longer any need to use animals for work. We have technology that can replace them. It's similar to using children to work in factories. Two hundred years ago, factory owners got rich by using children. Nowadays, people still get rich by using animals to do work for them. The problem is that the animals have no one to represent them and protect their rights. Even though animals work hard for us, they are often abandoned when they get sick or too old to work. They **suffer**. In short, I strongly believe that using animals for work is an old-fashioned and **cruel** practice.

Host: Thank you, Ms Johnson. Dr Kuryan – your introduction, please.

Dr Kuryan: Thank you. It's true that animals have helped our civilization develop. Camels and horses helped us carry goods across huge distances. Dogs helped us hunt and protected us from wild animals. Humans don't have the skills or strength to do these jobs. I want to argue that, in many developing countries, poor people still need animals to survive.

These are people who can't afford cars, house alarms or expensive machines. Another point is that not all animal use is **abuse**. On the contrary, without humans, these domesticated animals would not have been able to survive. They need us to take care of them. There are many animal lovers around the world who work in animal shelters and help animals. There are laws that stop animal suffering. And people give a lot of money to animal charities and organizations that help save wildlife. At the same time, there are still millions of children in the world who don't get this kind of treatment. They go without food or clothing. I strongly believe that, in a modern society, people often care more about animals than they do about poor people.

Host: Thank you both for your arguments! Now, let's hear from our listeners …

 1.2

Hello, and thank you all for coming. I know that you're all busy students and I appreciate that you're here today.

So, what do you think of when you hear the words *climate change*? You probably think about warmer temperatures, floods, droughts, huge storms … and maybe polar bears. That's what I'm going to talk about today – the polar bear and the human **threats** to this beautiful, powerful, majestic animal.

It's widely known that polar bears are now an **endangered species**. There are only about 26,000 polar bears in the world today and it's believed that most of them will be gone by 2050 if nothing changes. There are several threats to polar bears.

The biggest threat is the loss of sea ice **habitat**. Climate change **damages** the sea ice, which polar bears **depend on** for survival.

The disappearing ice has several negative effects. For example, polar bears have problems searching for seals, their main **source** of food. Polar bears need to stand on ice to hunt for seals. So when there isn't enough ice, the bears become hungry.

A second threat is contact between humans and polar bears. When the sea ice **melts**, polar bears have to spend more time on land. When polar bears go near towns, people sometimes kill the bears to protect themselves.

A third human threat to polar bears is industrial development, such as oil production and shipping. As the ice disappears, the ocean is growing. This means more oil production in the Arctic and an increased threat of oil spills. Contact with oil will kill polar bears. And the oil ships are also dangerous to polar bears.

However, there is good news: it may not be too late to save the polar bear. Here's what people are already doing.

First, Arctic communities are trying to reduce contact between humans and polar bears. More lights in public places, electric fences and warning plans when bears enter towns all help to protect both polar bears and humans.

Second, governments have made laws which limit the amount of oil production in the Arctic. And environmental groups are creating plans to make Arctic shipping safer.

Third, people are trying to stop climate change. And you can, too. To help save polar bears, you should use less electricity and petrol. And you could tell government leaders your opinion about climate change. It might also be a good idea to get involved with organizations which are working to save polar bears.

So, to summarize, the main threat to polar bears is loss of habitat due to climate change. Related threats are human contact and industrial development. If people don't make changes quickly, polar bears may disappear.

 1.3

1 First, Arctic communities are trying to reduce contact between humans and polar bears.

2 Second, governments have made laws which limit the amount of oil production in the Arctic.

3 So, to summarize, the main threat to polar bears is loss of habitat due to climate change.

🔊 1.4

… beautiful, powerful, majestic …

🔊 1.5

… warmer temperatures, floods, droughts, huge storms …

🔊 1.6

1 large, white, strong

2 pandas, sea turtles, chimpanzees, tigers

3 human contact, climate change, industrial development

4 more lights, electric fences, warning plans

1.7

It's often said that it's cruel to use animals for entertainment. However, I would like to argue against this idea. I know that many animal lovers would disagree with me, but let me explain my point of view.

First of all, keeping animals in zoos helps protect them. For example, many species, such as the giant panda and the snow leopard, are endangered in the wild, so they are safer in zoos. Another point is that zoos have an important educational role. For instance, children can see animals up close. When I was a child, my father took me to the zoo. I learned about exotic animals and I also learned to care about animals. Modern zoos have improved their conditions. Animals are no longer kept in small cages and zoos have large areas where animals can feel as if they are in their natural habitat.

To summarize, zoos help protect animals and educate us. In short, modern zoos are comfortable, safe places for wild animals. In conclusion, I believe that we should help zoos by visiting them and donating money.

 1.8

1   First of all, keeping animals in zoos helps protect them.

2   For example, many species, such as the giant panda and the snow leopard, are endangered in the wild.

3   Another point is that zoos have an important educational role.

4   To summarize, zoos help protect animals and educate us.

5   In short, modern zoos are comfortable, safe places for wild animals.

UNIT 2

▶ Blowing in the wind: offshore wind farms

Narrator: We humans use a lot of energy and some traditional energy sources are running out. Where can we find alternative energy sources? These days, one popular source is wind.

In 2013 the largest offshore wind farm opened here in the open sea.

It's called the London Array and it's located about 12 miles from the southeast coast of England.

How was it possible to build this giant wind farm in the water?

This was the answer.

Discovery is a special ship that can rise completely out of the water on giant 'legs'. It made a safe building area in the middle of the sea possible.

And it could hold all the parts to build each wind turbine.

These huge pieces of the turbine look like airplane wings. They were designed to get as much energy as possible, even from light winds.

But as you can imagine, they were difficult to assemble, especially in windy weather.

It took a team effort. Everything had to line up perfectly.

Success!

Each one of these wind turbines is almost 400 feet across. That's 120 metres, about as big as the London Eye. And they built 175 of them.

Every turbine can provide power for 3,000 homes. So now, because of the London Array wind farm, over half a million homes in England have clean electricity.

 2.1

1   Today I want to explain some alternative solutions.

2   As we all know, in order to grow plants we need water and sunlight.

3   I think that desert farms might be a very interesting way to farm in the future.

4   If you add the nutrients to water, you can grow fruit and vegetables in water.

 2.2

Good morning. Today I want to explain some **alternative solutions** which may help reduce some of the problems related to climate change. The first solution uses solar energy to grow food in the desert. First of all, I'll explain how farming in the desert works. Then, we'll briefly discuss how this type of farming could solve some of the **environmental** problems we are now facing. We'll discuss some possible problems with this **system**.

So, how does it work? As we all know, in order to grow plants we need water and sunlight. There's a lot of sunlight in the desert, but very little water. Scientists have combined solar energy with a farming technology called hydroponics. *Hydroponics* means growing plants in water. Plants don't need to grow in the ground, but they *do* need nutrients to help them grow. Nutrients are like food for the plants. So, if you add the nutrients to water, you can grow fruit and vegetables in water. NASA scientists have been developing this method of growing food because it could allow us to grow food in any climate – in Antarctica, the Sahara desert or even on Mars. You might ask how this method of growing plants helps with the problem of climate change. I mean, after all, it uses fresh water, which is a **limited resource**.

An Australian company, Sundrop Farms, combined hydroponics with solar energy. Traditional farming uses between 60 and 80 percent of our planet's fresh water. However, Sundrop Farms doesn't use fresh water. It uses seawater. Sundrop Farms is only 100 metres from the shore. A line of mirrors reflects heat from the sun onto a pipe which has oil inside. The hot oil in the pipe heats up seawater, which is kept in special containers. When the seawater reaches 160 °C, the steam **provides** electricity. Some of the hot water is used to heat the greenhouse during the cold desert nights. The plants grow in the greenhouse – a building with glass walls and a glass ceiling. The rest of the heated water goes to a desalination plant. Desalination is when we remove the salt from seawater to create drinkable water – that is, water which is clean and safe to drink. The desalination plant can produce up to 10,000 litres of fresh water every day. The farmer adds nutrients to this fresh water and then grows fruit and vegetables.

To summarize, solar energy removes the salt from the seawater and the fresh water is then used inside the greenhouse, where the plants are growing. Many people around the world are really excited about this technology. So far, Australian farms have grown tomatoes, peppers and cucumbers using hydroponics. Many supermarkets are interested in buying these vegetables because they're grown without pesticides or other chemicals. Some people think hydroponics is the perfect solution to the world food **crisis**.

Finally, the desert farms use solar energy and not fossil fuels, thus their negative effect on the environment is minimal. Now, of course, the future of hydroponics is unknown. But I think that desert farms might be a very interesting way to farm in the future. Now let's discuss some of the problems ...

🔊 2.3

An Australian company, Sundrop Farms, combined hydroponics with solar energy. Traditional farming uses between 60 and 80 percent of our planet's fresh water. However, Sundrop Farms doesn't use fresh water. It uses seawater. Sundrop Farms is only

100 metres from the shore. A line of mirrors reflects heat from the sun onto a pipe which has oil inside. The hot oil in the pipe heats up seawater, which is kept in special containers. When the seawater reaches 160 °C, the steam from this process provides electricity. Some of the hot water is used to heat the greenhouse during the cold desert nights. The plants grow in the greenhouse – a building with glass walls and a glass ceiling. The rest of the heated water goes to a desalination plant. Desalination is when we remove the salt from seawater to create drinkable water – that is, water which is clean and safe to drink. The desalination plant can produce up to 10,000 litres of fresh water every day. The farmer adds nutrients to this fresh water and then grows fruit and vegetables.

To summarize, solar energy removes the salt from the seawater and the fresh water is then used inside the greenhouse, where the plants are growing. Many people around the world are really excited about this technology. So far, Australian farms have grown tomatoes, peppers and cucumbers using hydroponics. Many supermarkets are interested in buying these vegetables because they're grown without pesticides or other chemicals. Some people think hydroponics is the perfect solution to the world food crisis.

Finally, the desert farms use solar energy and not fossil fuels, thus their negative effect on the environment is minimal. Now, of course, the future of hydroponics is unknown. But I think that desert farms might be a very interesting way to farm in the future. Now let's discuss some of the problems ...

🔊 2.4

1 Today I want to explain some alternative solutions which may help reduce some of the problems related to climate change.

2 NASA scientists have been developing this method of growing food because it could allow us to grow food in any climate.

3 I think that desert farms might be a very interesting way to farm in the future.

🔊 2.5

Host: Welcome to today's debate on the advantages and disadvantages of nuclear energy. Some people think that nuclear power is an environmentally friendly source of energy because it creates less pollution than traditional power plants. However, the **opponents** of nuclear energy believe that it has more dangers than **benefits**. Debating this issue today are Emma Martinez and Jack Sullivan. Thank you for joining us today to share your opinions about this important issue.

Emma: Thank you. I want to argue that there are many problems with nuclear power. It may be true that there are very few accidents caused by nuclear plants, but if there is an accident, then it will be huge and it will have **long-term** effects on the environment. For example, after the Fukushima nuclear **disaster** in Japan, the government had to tell people to leave their homes because of the possibility of radiation. The radioactive material spread to water and food, such as tea, milk, beef and fish. For months after the accident, the Fukushima plant was dangerous. People will not be able to live in the nearby area for the next 20 years. This is the big **risk** of building a nuclear power plant. In my opinion, it's irresponsible for governments to allow nuclear power plants to be built near cities. They're just too dangerous.

Jack: I have to disagree. I think we should look at the bigger picture. Some people are worried that nuclear power is a big risk. And yet there are hundreds of nuclear power plants all over the world and there have only been three major nuclear accidents in the last 30 years. In fact, research shows that many more people die while working with coal, natural gas and hydropower – that is, electricity powered by water. On top of that, nuclear power is the most environmentally friendly and the most sustainable source of energy. In other words, it doesn't damage the environment and there will always be enough of it. A nuclear power plant does not **pollute** the air, it's relatively cheap and it can provide a huge amount of electricity to our cities. And of course, our cities are growing ...

Emma: I'm sorry, can I interrupt? Some people say that nuclear energy doesn't pollute the air, but that's not completely true. It takes many years to build a nuclear power plant. During this time, hundreds of machines work day and night and pollute the air in the area. I don't think it's necessary to build nuclear power plants when we have safer and more environmentally friendly energy sources, such as solar and wind energy. They're cheaper and they're unlimited sources of energy. Also they're more **affordable** for most countries, when compared with nuclear power. Building a nuclear power plant is not a solution for poor or developing countries.

Jack: I'm not sure about that. I think that building nuclear power plants is the perfect solution for many poorer countries. Yes, it might be expensive to build the plant, but once the nuclear plant is there, the cost of the production of energy is very low. Plus, the country can sell the electricity to its neighbours and improve its economy. It's a long-term solution. And it makes a country less dependent on oil and gas. At the moment, whenever oil or gas prices go up, it's the poor countries and poor people who suffer. Some people think that solar and wind energy are greener than nuclear energy. But I don't think that's accurate. Wind turbines are not exactly friendly for birds, not to mention that solar panels and wind turbines take up a lot of space. They're also very expensive and don't last as long as a nuclear power plant. In short, wind and solar energy can't solve the problem of climate change and they aren't a good solution for poor countries.

Host: Thank you both very much. Let's take some questions from the audience ...

UNIT 3

▶ The air travel revolution

Narrator: In the past 50 years we've done the impossible – we've made the world smaller. Today we can travel from continent to continent in no time. Paris and London are closer than ever before.
North America and Europe are almost neighbours. And South America and Asia are less than a day away from each other.
Trips that used to happen once in a lifetime now happen weekly for many business people.
How have we done this? By taking to the air.
Aeroplanes have clearly revolutionized transportation.
Military planes travel faster than the speed of sound.
Commercial planes, like the Airbus A380 and the Boeing 747, are much bigger than houses. More people travel by air than ever in history.
The airspace over London, for example, is among the busiest and most crowded in the world.
Every day 3,500 flights take place overhead. And that's just one city.
In 2016, about 3.7 billion people travelled by plane. And that number will likely continue to grow.
The sky has become a place for us to work, rest and play.
And right now, around the world, over a million people are travelling in the air above us.

🔊 3.1

1 There has been an increase in motorcycle accidents over the past five years.
2 Airlines are always looking for new ways to increase the safety of their planes.

🔊 3.2

1 There's a detailed record of each plane crash.
2 A machine called a 'black box' records everything the pilot and co-pilot say during a flight.
3 Some cities don't permit cycling on the pavement.
4 I'm sorry, but you need an employee parking permit to park in this garage.
5 The company presents an award for road safety to the safest city.
6 He received a new car as a present from his parents.

🔊 3.3

Host: Have you ever been afraid of flying? Do you feel **scared** when you sit on a plane? Are you stressed when there's turbulence? If so, you may have aerophobia. The word *aerophobia* comes from the Greek and it **consists of** two parts: *aero*, which means 'flight' or 'air', and *phobia*, which means 'fear'. People with aerophobia experience **extreme** fear or panic when they sit on a plane. In today's programme, we'll discuss some steps which you can take to reduce this fear. With me today is Mark Knowling. Mark used to be a flight attendant who was afraid of flying. He has written a book about his experience and often gives presentations to help other people deal with their phobias. Can you tell us more about your experience, Mark?

Mark: Yes, sure. So I took a flight attendant's course right after college. My goal was to see the world and I thought it would be a good job for me. I learned a lot more than I expected from the course. During the training, we studied a lot about air **safety**, but there were also lectures about plane **crashes**. The instructors would tell us horrible stories of serious problems – broken engines, birds hitting the aircraft, hijackings and even stories of planes crashing in the middle of the desert or in the ocean.

Host: That's terrible!

Mark: No, I don't think so. They were trying to make us take the job seriously. They would also discuss the research done by air crash investigators to help us understand the reasons behind air crashes. There's

a detailed record of each crash, which investigators check carefully.

Host: But for you, I suppose this training had the opposite effect. How did it influence you? Did it make you afraid of flying?

Mark: Uh-huh, the course had a strong impact on me. I actually became very scared of being on a plane. When I told my colleagues about it, they just laughed. They couldn't believe that I had completed the flight attendant training and now I was afraid to get on a plane. What was I supposed to do? I decided to research it online and I read stories about people who managed to control their fear of flying.

Host: Can it be cured?

Mark: Actually, like any phobia, there's not always a **cure** for it, but you can decrease its effects on your life. You need to have the right attitude. You can achieve anything if you concentrate and stay positive. The advice I got was very useful, but it was a challenge and it took me a long time to get over my fear.

🔊 3.4

Host: Can you share some advice with our listeners?

Mark: Of course. Well, the first method to reduce your fear is to learn more about how planes work. For example, many people believe that without the engines, the plane will simply fall down from the sky, but that isn't true. The plane will stay up because its wings push against the air. A plane can fly without the engines, and a well-trained pilot will be able to control it without power. All pilots learn how to fly without the engines.

Host: What about turbulence? Whenever I fly, I get very scared during turbulence.

Mark: Well, turbulence can be dangerous, of course. However, most turbulence is completely normal and won't cause any trouble, so you shouldn't be afraid of it. The only situation where it can cause problems is when the aircraft is already damaged or during a storm. But, as you know, airlines study the weather and won't carry passengers if they think the weather conditions aren't safe for flying.

Host: Is there any other advice that you can give?

Mark: Understanding where the emergency exits are may help you relax. Not knowing where an exit is and feeling that you're in a closed space can make you afraid. Finally, to reduce the fear of flying, you should **avoid** watching movies about plane crashes or other accidents. Some researchers say that aerophobia is caused by people watching too many disaster movies. I think we often forget that, compared to the many forms of transport that we use every day, air transport is actually very safe.

Host: In what way?

Mark: Well, there's research which **compares** the number of accidents per number of miles travelled on each form of transport. We can see that by far the safest form of travel is air transport, and the most dangerous is using a motorcycle. In recent years, there has been a significant decrease in the number of plane crashes. In contrast, cars are considerably more dangerous.

Host: Really? I didn't know that. Thank you for your advice, Mark. You can let us know what you think about air safety and share your stories by going to our website at www …

 3.5

1 The course was a lot more challenging than I expected.

2 We can see that by far the most affordable form of transport is walking.

3 The risks of driving a car are considerably more significant than those of flying.

4 For me, flying is much more comfortable than travelling by train.

5 Taking a train is definitely more relaxing than driving.

6 Using the underground is a lot faster than travelling by bus at rush hour.

7 Driving is considerably more expensive than walking.

8 Cycling is absolutely the healthiest form of transport.

 3.6

Hello, everyone. Thank you for being here today. Welcome to the first meeting of Wheels to Work. As you know, the goal of this group is to make our city more bicycle-friendly. Specifically, we'd like to make it easier for people to cycle to work. Cycling to work is good for the environment and it provides great exercise. And personally, I think it's a lot of fun!

I'm hoping that we can work together to **solve** the problems which can make it difficult for city residents to cycle to work. Today I'm going to talk about a few of those problems and share some ideas for solving them.

So, the biggest issue is safety. A lot of people would love to cycle to work, but they're scared – they feel that it's just too dangerous. This is because there's a lot of traffic during rush hour, when most people

drive to or from work, and there's very little space for cyclists. Many of the cycle lanes we have are too narrow and some of the busiest streets don't even have cycle lanes. What's more, many drivers don't have **respect** for cyclists. Cars sometimes even drive in the cycle lanes to **pass** other cars. Of course, if a car hits a bicycle, it's going to **injure** or even kill the cyclist.

A second issue is storage. Many people don't have a safe place to put their bicycles while they're at work. They worry that if they leave their bicycle outside, it'll get stolen. Also, it'll get wet when it rains and might get damaged over time.

A third problem is that, for some people, cycling to work isn't **convenient**. Maybe they live far from their job or maybe they sometimes work late and don't want to cycle home in the dark. And a lot of people don't like to cycle in the rain. What if you cycle to work and then later it starts raining? From my own experience, I can tell you that it's pretty terrible to ride home during a storm.

So, those are three of the biggest issues: safety, storage and convenience.

 3.7

Now I'd like to share some possible solutions. First, to improve safety, I'd suggest that police officers give big **fines** to drivers who **break the law** by driving in a cycle lane.

Also, I'd like to see wider cycle lanes to allow more bicycles to pass at the same time. We should also add cycle lanes to busy streets which don't have them yet. These proposals would **prevent** cars from hitting cyclists and would save lives.

As for the issue of storage, I think that city parking garages ought to create special parking sections for bicycles. This would keep bicycles safe and dry while people are working.

Finally, convenience. In my opinion, we should make it easier to take bicycles on public transport. For example, we could put cycle racks on the outside of buses. That way, people wouldn't have to cycle at night or in bad weather. And people who live far from work could cycle part of the way to work and take public transport the rest of the way. As a result, more people could cycle to work.

Well, thank you again for listening to my ideas. I hope this is the beginning of a conversation about how we can make this a great city for cyclists!

🔊 3.8

A: I'm really surprised by these statistics. I didn't know that eating while driving is dangerous. I don't think the government should do anything about it. Personally, I eat fast food in my car a few times a week and I've never had an accident. And I'm not convinced that driving while eating is a big problem. Have you ever eaten while driving?

B: No, I haven't. We should take this really seriously. I think it would be better if they closed drive-through restaurants. This is because they only encourage drivers to buy food and eat it while they drive. How can you focus on the road if you're holding a big burger in your hand? It seems dangerous to me. What do you think?

C: I completely agree. I think it would be much better if drivers weren't allowed to eat or drink while they drive. From my own experience, I can tell you that it can be very dangerous. Last week, I bought some coffee and something to eat on the way to work. As I was driving, I had to brake suddenly and I spilled hot coffee over my legs. I almost lost control of the car. I think the police should give heavy fines if they see someone doing it.

D: OK, I understand, but it might be very difficult for the police to see drivers eating, especially if they're driving fast. The best thing would be to have more cameras on the roads to record what drivers are doing. The reason for this is the police can check the videos to see who's eating, who's texting and so on. Then, I'd suggest that the police give the drivers points on their licence. If the driver has a lot of points, the police should take their car away for a few months.

UNIT 4

▶ **Chinese moon cakes**

Narrator: The Mid-Autumn festival is celebrated by Chinese people across the world. It is traditionally a harvest festival, to celebrate the rice and wheat that has been grown that year, and it takes place on the full moon. People get together with family and friends to watch the moon, admire the lights and eat the traditional sweet of this festival – moon cakes. Moon cakes are rarely made at home because the recipe is quite complicated. Most people prefer to buy their moon cakes from a shop or a hotel. Here at the famous Peninsula Hotel in Hong Kong, chef Yip Wing Wah shows how the cakes are made.

First, he makes the filling for the moon cakes. Here he is mixing butter with sugar. To that he will add other ingredients to make a thick, sweet paste. Now the chef is taking a yellow ball of filling and wrapping it in a thin layer of pastry. Moon cakes can have a number of different fillings. For example, in more traditional recipes, the filling is made from sweet red beans, and you will find half of a salty duck egg inside that.

Next, the chef takes a special wooden mould and shapes each moon cake, one at a time. Each moon cake has a decoration on top of it. Many different patterns are used on moon cakes, including flower patterns or Chinese letters. The decoration on top is brushed with egg yolk. When baked in the oven this will turn a lovely golden brown.

Then, the moon cakes must be left for a day or two. The butter from the filling will go into the pastry layer and make it soft and delicious.

And here we have it, a sweet treat perfect with a cup of refreshing tea, on the night of the full moon.

🔊 4.1

This Sunday on *Book of the Week*, we interview Dr Kevin Lee, the well-known anthropologist and author. In this podcast, he will tell us of his love for Cultural anthropology and we'll discuss whether traditions are adapting to the modern world or dying out.

🔊 4.2

Host: Welcome to this week's book review. In the studio with me is Dr Kevin Lee, professor of Anthropology and author of the best-selling book *Changing Traditions in the Modern World*. First of all, could you tell us what anthropologists study and what your own area of interest is?

Dr Lee: That's a good question! Anthropology, in a general sense, is the study of humanity. I know that's not very exact. That's why we have many types of Anthropology, like Linguistic anthropology and **Social** anthropology. My speciality is Cultural anthropology. I study different cultures around the world and how social and **political** changes affect these cultures.

Host: And when did you first become interested in Anthropology?

Dr Lee: I grew up in a **multicultural** home. My mother is American and my father is Korean. They were both English teachers, so we travelled a lot.

As a child, I lived in Japan, Thailand and Egypt. That's why I decided to study Anthropology. Growing up in different cultures helps you realize that customs and traditions are often local. Things that are acceptable in one culture can be completely unacceptable in another. However, despite some differences between cultures, I have noticed that there are often more similarities than differences between people.

Host: And do traditions change?

Dr Lee: Absolutely! Customs and traditions change all the time. Some traditions **die out** because our way of life changes, but most traditions adapt.

Host: As I understand it, that's one of the main points of your latest book.

Dr Lee: Yes. My book is about the effect of modern technology on traditions around the world. It's well known that things such as electricity, the telephone and television have changed our lives significantly. The introduction of these inventions into our lives has changed many of our customs. For example, in the past, families spent time playing board games or listening to the radio in the evening. These activities would deepen family relationships. Now, due to developments in technology, people spend more time **interacting** with other people over the internet.

Host: Is that a bad thing?

Dr Lee: I don't think so. There are people who complain about the changes that technology has brought to our lives. Personally, I think these changes are fine. We still spend time interacting with other people, but it's not always face-to-face.

Host: In your book, you discuss how technology has changed the way we celebrate important holidays.

Dr Lee: That's right. A simple example is sending cards or messages. In the past, people sent each other cards to celebrate important events, like an **anniversary** or a new baby. But now, more people send messages through social networking sites or by text or email. Another example of changing customs is holiday food. A few **generations** ago, people spent a lot of time and effort preparing special meals for **celebrations**. It was usually the women who did this. Some dishes could take up to a week to prepare. But now we don't have to work so hard. This is because we have modern kitchens and supermarket food. We don't have to spend endless hours making our own butter or bread any more. Everything is quicker and easier now.

Host: Hmm ... I remember my grandmother working for days to make food. She had a huge cookery book which she got from her grandmother. Everything had to be exactly as it was when she was a little girl.

Dr Lee: That's a good example of a tradition which has been replaced by technology. You can find any recipe you want on the internet. This means that many people don't need cookery books any more. Another thing is that many families now go out instead of cooking at home. In India, for example, families hire catering companies to provide food for weddings or special occasions. In the United States, at Thanksgiving, which is one of the biggest celebrations, many families go to restaurants because they don't want to spend their holiday working in the kitchen.

Host: So people do continue their tradition of eating a special meal – they just do it in a different way.

Dr Lee: Yes. Traditions don't always die out – but customs and traditions do change and adapt to the modern world.

 4.3

1 Anthropology, in a general sense, is the study of humanity. I know that's not very exact. That's why we have many types of Anthropology, like Linguistic anthropology and Social anthropology.

2 Some traditions die out because our way of life changes.

3 Now, due to developments in technology, people spend more time interacting with other people over the internet.

4 But now we don't have to work so hard. This is because we have modern kitchens and supermarket food.

5 In the United States, at Thanksgiving, which is one of the biggest celebrations, many families go to restaurants because they don't want to spend their holiday working in the kitchen.

🔊 4.4

I study different cultures around the world and how social and political changes affect these cultures.

🔊 4.5

1 My book is about the effect of modern technology on traditions around the world.

2 People spent a lot of time and effort preparing special meals.

3 Growing up in different cultures helps you realize that customs and traditions are often local.

4 We still spend time interacting with other people, but it's not always face-to-face.

5 In the past, people sent each other cards to celebrate important events, like an anniversary or a new baby.

6 Traditions don't always die out – but customs and traditions do change and adapt to the modern world.

🔊 4.6

Gabriela: So, our assignment is to discuss customs which have been changing recently – you know, how modern lifestyles have changed people's **behaviour**. Any ideas?

Yildiz: Hmm … Let me think. Well, holidays are one kind of custom. Can you think of any holidays which have changed?

David: Oh, don't talk about holidays! It reminds me that Mother's Day is in two days and I haven't bought a gift for my mum yet.

Gabriela: Yeah, I haven't either. Who has time for shopping when we have so much work to do?

David: I agree. I get tired of shopping for gifts. I actually don't know why we have to get gifts for every little holiday. Wouldn't our mothers be just as happy if we just spent time with them – you know, made it a special **event**, like taking them out to lunch at a nice restaurant? How did this whole gift giving for every holiday tradition get started, anyway? It seems silly to me.

Gabriela: That's it! There's our topic! How holidays have become too **commercial**.

🔊 4.7

Yildiz: Hold on, too commercial? I disagree. I like giving gifts. I think that it shows that you were thinking of someone.

David: Because you went out and got someone some chocolate or jewellery or a scarf or something at the last minute? Everyone knows that people usually buy gifts because it's an **obligation**, not because they really want to.

Yildiz: Well, you have to spend time thinking about the gift and get something **thoughtful**, you know, **personal**. Like maybe the new book by their favourite author.

Gabriela: I see your point. But I'm not convinced because then you have to spend money … money which could be spent on more important things. Also, all that time you spent shopping you could have instead spent with the person you're shopping for.

David: I couldn't agree more. And it's not just holidays which are a problem – personally, I think we give too many gifts for other special **occasions**, too. Like when my sister **graduated** from university last year, she got lots of gifts. And money, too. The focus was all on opening gifts. I've heard that when people receive more than a few gifts, they usually can't even remember who gave them which gift. Instead, why not write letters of advice for the future? That would be more special.

Gabriela: That's a great idea!

Yildiz: Sorry, I don't agree. I doubt that graduates would be happy if we changed that custom! I think that graduation gifts are practical. Don't young people need some gifts and money for starting their new life? And they can always look at the gift and think of the person who gave it to them. I think it's a nice custom.

Gabriela: I'm still really not convinced. I mean …

🔊 4.8

Gabriela: So, our assignment is to discuss customs which have been changing recently – you know, how modern lifestyles have changed people's behaviour. Any ideas?

Yildiz: Hmm … Let me think. Well, holidays are one kind of custom. Can you think of any holidays which have changed?

David: Oh, don't talk about holidays! It reminds me that Mother's Day is in two days and I haven't bought a gift for my mum yet.

Gabriela: Yeah, I haven't either. Who has time for shopping when we have so much work to do?

David: I agree. I get tired of shopping for gifts. I actually don't know why we have to get gifts for every little holiday. Wouldn't our mothers be just as happy if we just spent time with them – you know, made it a special event, like taking them out to lunch at a nice restaurant? How did this whole gift giving for every holiday tradition get started, anyway? It seems silly to me.

Gabriela: That's it! There's our topic! How holidays have become too commercial.

Yildiz: Hold on, too commercial? I disagree. I like giving gifts. I think that it shows that you were thinking of someone.

David: Because you went out and got someone some chocolate or jewellery or a scarf or something at the last minute? Everyone knows that people usually buy gifts because it's an obligation, not because they really want to.

Yildiz: Well, you have to spend time thinking about the gift and get something thoughtful, you know, personal. Like maybe the new book by their favourite author.

Gabriela: I see your point. But I'm not convinced because then you have to spend money ... money which could be spent on more important things. Also, all that time you spent shopping you could have instead spent with the person you're shopping for.

David: I couldn't agree more. And it's not just holidays which are a problem – personally, I think we give too many gifts for other special occasions, too. Like when my sister graduated from university last year, she got lots of gifts. And money, too. The focus was all on opening gifts. I've heard that when people receive more than a few gifts, they usually can't even remember who gave them which gift. Instead, why not write letters of advice for the future? That would be more special.

Gabriela: That's a great idea!

Yildiz: Sorry, I don't agree. I doubt that graduates would be happy if we changed that custom! I think that graduation gifts are practical. Don't young people need some gifts and money for starting their new life? And they can always look at the gift and think of the person who gave it to them. I think it's a nice custom.

Gabriela: I'm still really not convinced. I mean ...

🔊 4.9

1 I couldn't agree more.

2 How did this whole gift giving for every holiday tradition get started, anyway? It seems silly to me.

3 I agree. I get tired of shopping for gifts.

4 I disagree. I like giving gifts.

5 But I'm not convinced because then you have to spend money ... money which could be spent on more important things.

6 Instead, why not write letters of advice for the future? That would be more special.

7 Sorry, I don't agree. I doubt that graduates would be happy if we changed that custom!

🔊 4.10

I completely agree that holidays have become too commercial.

I absolutely disagree that we should stop giving gifts on Mother's Day.

I really think that we should give fewer gifts.

UNIT 5

 Childhood obesity

Narrator: There are now three times as many people in the world who are obese than there were in 1975. These days you are more likely to live in a country where being overweight or obese kills more people than being underweight. The problems can begin in childhood, when bad diet choices and not enough exercise become habits. Across the world, 19% of children between the ages of 5 and 19 are overweight or obese. In the UK, people are looking for ways to deal with the problem from childhood. They are looking at what happens during the school day. This report shows how good teachers can help.

Mr Clark: One, two, good steps, lovely, and again!

Reporter: Laurence Clark is a PE teacher on a mission, trying to revolutionize his lessons to encourage the kids to be more active.

Pupil 1: When you get fitter you also get healthier, so you can get more muscles what make them stronger.

Reporter: I bet you like eating sweets and chocolates.

Pupil 2: Only on Saturday, my mum says.

Reporter: But with 1 in 10 children in the UK now obese, Mr Clark believes his role is now more important than ever.

Mr Clark: If we can instil that confidence and get them moving properly, and get that confidence about their body and self-efficacy, then I feel if they ... as they get older, they're more inclined to lead that healthy lifestyle, especially when they get to secondary school and so on.

Narrator: So teaching children good exercise habits can help. But eating habits are equally important. A recent study found that only 1.6% of children's packed lunches were as healthy as the meals provided by schools. The healthy boxes all contained the traditional sandwich with a protein filling, such as meat or egg, and some salad. But 98.4% of parents are filling lunch boxes with too many snack foods and sugary drinks. Vegetables or salad were found in only 1 in 5. Salty snacks, such as crisps, were found in 60% of packed lunches. The researchers understood that many find it difficult to pack healthy meals for their children because of cost, lack of time or demands from their children. But, they said parents must control what their children are eating at lunch, for example by weighing out small amounts. If adults do not do something to help children control their weight soon, it looks certain that health problems caused by being obese will continue to increase.

🔊 5.1

Host: Today we're talking about the key to a long and happy life. Recent studies of people who live to be 100 years old have shown that a healthy diet and exercise may not be enough. In fact, many of the people who celebrate their hundredth birthday have not eaten a healthy diet and have never exercised regularly. This has led many people to believe that our lifestyles are not important. What's most important is that we have good genes. It seems that if you have the right genes, then you'll live for a long time, whatever you do.

🔊 5.2

Host: So, new research shows that having a healthy lifestyle is not the most important thing if you want to live a long life. We asked four people on the street for their reactions to this news.

A: I think it's great news! Most people think that if they eat healthy food and exercise a lot, they'll live forever. These people never drink coffee or sugary drinks. They spend hours **working out** in the gym or doing yoga. And none of this matters if you have the wrong genes. I think that the key to a healthy life is to enjoy yourself. If you focus all your energy on what to do and what not to do, you'll be unhappy eventually. There's no question that happy people live longer. I'd much rather go out and have a pizza with friends than spend time in the gym. I'm really happy about this new research!

B: This research **proves** what I've known for a long time. It's ridiculous to get too worried about healthy eating and exercise! My grandfather lived until he was 95, even though he never exercised. He ate lots of sugar and never ate vegetables. He was brought up in a different world. He had different **habits**. He certainly never went to a gym. Yes, I'm sure that

genes are more important than our lifestyle. Of course, I'm not going to give up exercising or start eating fast food every day. The research shows I should stay in shape because it makes me feel better – but I won't allow fitness to take over my whole life.

C: Well, first of all, I prefer to exercise and eat well. What's wrong with being healthy? I also think that you won't know whether or not you have the right genes until you get sick. So why take the risk and be **unhealthy**? Also, don't forget that you might get the flu or a cold much more easily when you don't eat healthy food or exercise. I'd say that it's always better to have a healthy lifestyle. There's no doubt that bad health habits increase the chances of getting a serious **illness**.

D: Oh, that's great. So now we should all eat fast food and stop exercising? I mean I look around and I see **overweight** children everywhere. No matter how good their genes are, I'm sure that these children won't be able to enjoy a long and healthy life unless they give up crisps, chocolate bars, sugary drinks … Well, it's great that some people can live to be 100 and do whatever they want in their lives, but I prefer to be careful and take care of myself because I don't know if I have good genes!

🔊 5.3

I'm really surprised about that.
I'm really surprised about that.
I'm really surprised about that!

🔊 5.4

1 I'm really happy about this new research!
2 There's no question that happy people live longer.
3 It's ridiculous to get too worried about healthy eating and exercise!
4 He certainly never went to a gym.
5 There's no doubt that bad health habits increase the chances of getting a serious illness.

🔊 5.5

1 I think it's great news!
2 Oh, that's great.
3 What's wrong with being healthy?
4 So now we should all eat fast food and stop exercising?
5 I'd say that it's always better to have a healthy lifestyle.

6 Well, it's great that some people can live to be 100 and do whatever they want in their lives, but I prefer to be careful and take care of myself because I don't know if I have good genes!

🔊 5.6

Presenter 1: Do you have problems focusing on your work? Are you under a lot of **stress**? Do you want to get more exercise while trying something new and exciting? If so, it's time to take up taekwondo! Taekwondo is great exercise. And as we all know, exercise is good for your health. Taekwondo also has **mental** benefits – it has been shown to improve your **concentration**. In addition, it makes you feel good about yourself. This martial art was developed in Korea, and is now popular around the world. Whether you are looking for physical well-being, increased confidence or a life with less stress, *Black Belt Taekwondo* has it all. Sign up now for a free introductory class, starting on January the 15th.

Presenter 2: Would you like to improve your social life, your intellectual **performance**, your physical fitness and your team-building skills? Scientific research has proven that team sports offer all of these benefits. Join us and take advantage of the many benefits of team sports. We're a group of energetic adults of all ages who get together on Sunday afternoons to play football and we're always looking for new players to join in the fun. Whether you've been playing football for years or want to take up a new sport, you're welcome to **participate**. Everyone can play – you don't even need to try out! If you're interested in learning more about our group, check out our website at www.footballsundays.cup.com. Sign up today and you can be part of a team as early as this weekend! Hope to see you on the field soon!

Presenter 3: Hi, my name's Angie Stratton and I'm the director of CultureCycle. CultureCycle is a new concept in travel: educational fitness touring! We offer courses all over the world which combine learning with exercise and travel. Each course has an educational theme, such as Brazilian cooking or the history of Turkey. As a small group, we cycle from place to place, stopping for several days in each location to rest, **relax** and do some hands-on learning. Not only does this trip provide terrific exercise and a fascinating cultural experience, it's the best way to learn. There's no question that physical activity improves our memory and thinking skills – so after a few days of cycling, your brain will be ready to learn. So, be kind to your body and your mind and come with us on an amazing adventure you'll never forget!

Presenter 4: Are you interested in alternative **treatments**? Have you ever wanted to explore the secrets of traditional Chinese medicine? This spring, join our six-month course in acupuncture – a treatment for pain or illness which involves putting needles under the skin at special points on the body. The course covers the theory of acupuncture and practical skills in using needles. Acupuncture is known to **reduce** pain, but it's also a great alternative for people who want to lose weight in an easy way. Learn more about the course and visit us on our open house days on the first Saturday of every month.

UNIT 6

▶ **A helping hand**

Anna Werner (reporter): Ask first grader Holden Mora how his new hand works and he'll be happy to demonstrate.

Holden Mora: So when I bend my hand in like this, it closes. When I bend it like this, it opens.

Anna Werner: At seven years old, he's become an expert on the workings of this novel device made out of plastic for roughly $20.

Holden Mora: It's an amazing $20.

Anna Werner: It's an amazing $20.

Holden Mora: And normally, the materials cost a lot. About, like, $1,000.

Anna Werner: He's right. Children like Holden, born without hands or fingers, in his case the fingers on his left hand, often require custom prosthetic replacements costing thousands of dollars. But this inexpensive device was created by a college student using a 3D printer.

Jeff Powell: It builds it layer by layer.

Anna Werner: Senior Jeff Powell studies biomedical engineering at the University of North Carolina at Chapel Hill. He took on the project after learning about Holden from one of his professors.

Jeff Powell: OK, try that now.

Anna Werner: He used instructions posted on the internet, called the Cyborg Beast, then customized it. The 3D printer builds the parts in under 24 hours. And at the end, what you wind up with, is this.

Jeff Powell: Yes.

Anna Werner: Right.

Jeff Powell: Yes. So the way this works is it straps onto Holden's hand and onto the end of his forearm. When he moves his wrist in, the fingers close. When he moves his wrist out, the fingers open.

Anna Werner: And, do that again. Do they have grip strengths? So, oh, they actually do have grip strength.

Jeff Powell: Yes.

Anna Werner: His goal: for Holden to be able to do things the rest of us take for granted.

Jeff Powell: To be able to eat dinner while holding, you know, a knife and a fork at the same time. To be able to grab onto his scooter or his bike with two hands. Maybe even, you know, swing a baseball bat if we get it that strong enough. I don't want him to be limited by the condition that he was born with.

Anna Werner: So this isn't just about a hand for him, is it?

Jeff Powell: No, no. It's about enabling him to do anything that he wants to do.

Anna Werner: And the payoff for this amateur designer? When he picked up a cup, you were able to say to yourself, 'Hey, this worked.'

Jeff Powell: Yes, yes.

Anna Werner: That had to be a great moment.

Jeff Powell: Yes. It was nice to see it all pay off.

Anna Werner: Powell has now started a crowdfunding campaign to raise money so other kids can get the device too.

Holden Mora: Well, I'm actually really happy because I think it's true that once I get the best hand, they'll make more like it for those kids. And then they'll have the best kind of hand, too.

Anna Werner: Eleven more children are already waiting for their new hands. For CBS *This Morning*, Anna Werner, Chapel Hill, North Carolina.

🔊 6.1

Welcome to the Museum of Science! The exhibition that we're about to see is called *Discovering Medieval Science*. As some of you may know, the Middle Ages have often been called the 'Dark Ages'. During this tour, you will find out that they were not. The Middle Ages were an interesting time and they were full of **scientific** discoveries. During this time, inventions and **technology** from India, China, North Africa and the Middle East were brought to Europe.

Inventions and machines **designed** by medieval scholars made a great contribution to society and many are still in use today. And some of these inventions are very common. For example, the first fountain pen was made in 953 in Africa. Before then, people used bird feathers and ink to write with. This method would often leave your fingers and clothes covered with black ink. So the first fountain pen had a small container with ink inside and did not stain people's clothes or fingers while the user was writing. You can see a model of this fountain pen in Room 11B. In the same room, you'll find early examples of glasses. Glasses were **invented** in Italy in the thirteenth century. No one knows who invented them. The first glasses were held in front of the eyes or balanced on the nose. They were **developed** to help people with bad vision to read. But let's now move on to some other inventions.

In rooms 12A and 12B we have works by the great medieval engineer, al-Jazari. Al-Jazari lived in twelfth-century Turkey. His work *The Book of Knowledge of Ingenious Mechanical Devices* lists one hundred different machines with instructions and **diagrams** explaining how to build them. In this exhibition, you can see models of some of the **devices** which were designed by al-Jazari. Here, you can see his mechanical clocks. Water and weights make the clocks work. However, his most important invention was the crankshaft. The crankshaft is a long arm which allows machines to move in a straight line. It was first used for watering gardens and fields on farms. In more modern times, a crankshaft is used in car engines.

As we move along, you'll find one of the most important inventions of medieval times. This invention has changed the history of the world in ways that we can't even imagine. It's one of the four great inventions of Chinese culture: gunpowder. Gunpowder was invented in the ninth century by Chinese scientists who were trying to create a powder which would make you live forever. They weren't successful, of course, but their attempts led to the invention of fireworks and weapons. The first instructions on how to make gunpowder were written in the eleventh century by Zeng Gongliang, Ding Du and Yang Weide. The invention of gunpowder has changed the way we fight wars. It changed the outcome of many medieval battles and affected the history of the world. Many people think gunpowder is the most important invention in history. Now, let's move to the next room, which is all about medieval medicine ...

🔊 6.2

1 Inventions and technology from India, China, North Africa and the Middle East were brought to Europe.

2 The first glasses were held in front of the eyes or balanced on the nose.

3 The crankshaft is a long arm which allows machines to move in a straight line.

4 As we move along, you'll find one of the most important inventions of medieval times.

🔊 6.3

1 The Middle Ages were an interesting time and they were full of scientific discoveries.

2 Inventions and machines designed by medieval scholars made a great contribution to society and many are still in use today. And some of these inventions are very common.

3 Many people think gunpowder is the most important invention in history.

🔊 6.4

Good morning! In today's lecture I want to discuss an invention which has changed our lives. This **product** has made a huge difference in the way we work, travel, communicate and socialize with friends. Can you guess what it is? I'm talking here about mobile phone **apps**. The word *app* comes from *application*. Traditionally, applications were used in computers to help them perform better. However, with the invention of smartphones, the word *app* is used to refer to phone applications. In this lecture, we'll start by discussing the very first apps and their development. We will then discuss how apps have changed our lives. Finally, we'll focus on some of the most popular apps used by people today.

🔊 6.5

I'd like to start by talking a little bit about the first apps. These were included with each smartphone. These types of apps were placed in the phones to help **users access** the internet, check emails, send texts and so on. The first apps were designed to increase efficiency at work and **allow** people to access important information. However, it was the second generation of apps that really changed things. These were downloadable apps. Users simply downloaded apps from the internet and **installed** them on their phones. Since its introduction, the app market has grown far beyond anyone's expectations.

The first app store was opened in 2008. By 2011, it was reporting over 10 billion downloads and people were using apps more than internet browsers on their phones. And by 2017, an estimated 180 billion apps had been downloaded. These numbers have been growing ever since and they give us a good idea about how popular apps are and how quickly they've developed. People from all over the world use apps for entertainment, travel and communication. So, I'm going to briefly talk about how these apps have changed our lives.

It's hard to imagine life before smartphones and mobile phone apps – or, for those of us who are old enough, to remember it. But let's go ahead and make an attempt anyway. So, imagine for a moment that you're taking a road trip in the days before smartphones.

Weeks before the trip, you go to the bookstore or library to get some guidebooks about the places you're going to visit. A few days before you leave, you get some audio books to entertain you during the long trip. You go to a shop and buy some maps – yes, the paper kind. The day before the trip, you sit down at your computer and look up the directions and print them out. Then, you pack some of your favourite CDs to bring along. You also pack your camera – and your torch, in case your car breaks down. And you write down some phone numbers and addresses – of the friends you'll be visiting and the hotels where you'll be staying.

While you're driving, your passenger reads the directions to you and looks for street signs. If you get lost, you stop at a petrol station to ask for directions. You have to write them down on a piece of paper. OK, so I think you get the idea.

Now let's make a comparison with the same trip today. No books, no maps, no CDs, no lists of phone numbers, no friend giving you directions – the smartphone does it all! Think of the apps you'd use just for that one trip. You'd read reviews and book your hotel with a travel app. The GPS would replace the directions and maps and your friend in the front seat. Of course, a music app would replace the CDs and you could listen to podcasts, as well as audio books. And, of course, you wouldn't need to bring a camera or a torch. Yes, we've certainly made a lot of progress since the pre-smartphone days!

So, now I'd like to mention another important effect of the invention of apps. It has **created** a whole new IT sector. It is one of the fastest-growing **industries** and there is a great need for skilled software engineers.

But apps have also had some negative effects. For one thing, people have become more helpless because they're so dependent on their phones for information. For example, if they're in a place with no phone signal, they're not very good at asking for and following directions. And apps have made people less patient because they expect to have information immediately. In fact, a recent study found that 50 percent of smartphone users leave a web page if it doesn't load in 10 seconds.

OK, in the next part of the lecture, I'll discuss some of the most common apps in more detail …

🔊 6.6

I would like to present an invention which has made the way we organize our work easier. It's a simple invention and most of you have used it. It's a small yellow piece of paper which is known all over the world. It's the Post-it® note. A Post-it® note is a piece of paper with special glue on the back. Modern Post-it® notes can be any colour or shape. Post-it® notes are simple to use. You can stick them on anything and the note will stay in place. The notes can be easily removed from any surface. First, I am going to talk about the history of this invention. Then, I will explain how it has made a difference in our lives.

UNIT 7

▶ Interview with College of Art graduate Christopher Raeburn

Narrator: Christopher Raeburn is a fashion designer with a difference. His clothes are both extremely fashionable and good for the environment, too. He started making recycled fashion items from old military uniforms when he was at university. These days, his recycled brand, *Remade*, is a fashion success, and he is now making clothes from other spare military materials, such as parachute material.

Christopher Raeburn: I'm based here in London in the East End, Hackney Wick, but err … originally I'm from Kent in southeast England.

I … I never really set out to um to create an ethical or sustainable brand. For me it's just more about intelligent use of materials, it's about um the fact that I knew I wanted to do my production here in England and because I … I love the fabrics and I recycle the fabrics. Inherently, you've already got

a very sustainable brand you know because you are recycling, because you are doing your production because you are employing local people.

This season we're actually splitting the collection into three sections. We have the *Remade* that hopefully everyone knows and loves before, we've got our lightweight fabrics, you know the parachute and, erm … waterproof fabrics, but this season we're also working in a new British erm … section of the collection and that's very much focused on, erm … incredibly good quality British milled wools.

We're actually doing my London Fashion Week presentation at Aldwych Tube Station. It hasn't actually been used for proper underground, err … trains for 10 to 15 years now and so we'll be getting in and doing a very different event, erm … it'll be multimedia, I'll be presenting my new film. And for the first time I'll also be working with um models as well presenting the garments, erm … both men's- and womenswear.

Narrator: The ideas for Christopher's designs come firstly from the old fabric or piece of clothing he's recycling. Then he adds ideas he gets from other places. He's particularly interested in the military, adventure, outdoor activities and cultures that come from cold places, like the Inuit. He connects all these ideas in the different garments in each collection.

🔊 7.1

Clara: Do you have any ideas for our research project?

Adele: I've been looking for an interesting topic, but to be honest, I haven't come up with anything yet. Can you give me a hand?

Clara: Well, I've been reading about fashion of the future, new **designs**, new technology and all that.

Adele: Do you mean the kinds of clothes that we're going to be wearing in the future? I'm not really into fashion …

Clara: Actually, it's more about future **fabrics** and how we're going to use them.

Adele: Well?

Clara: OK. I've found out that there are designers who create eco-clothes.

Adele: Eco-clothes?

Clara: Yeah. They're clothes that are not only good for the community but also environmentally friendly.

The designers make sure that the clothes aren't made by people working in bad conditions. **Local** workshops are set up so that people can earn a good salary. And eco-friendly clothing typically helps protect the environment, too, apparently.

Adele: How do they work, exactly?

Clara: Well, there are fabrics that collect the energy from when you move. Then, the energy is **converted** into electricity.

Adele: Interesting. So, a few years from now, we'll probably be using this fabric to charge our phones, right?

Clara: Well, as long as you keep moving, yes!

Adele: That reminds me of **smart** fabrics. I saw an exhibit about them at the science festival. Some scientists are working on fabrics which can kill bacteria and regulate body temperature.

Clara: Wow! How does that work?

Adele: Well, these fabrics keep your body temperature the same in any kind of weather. And I read that they can be used to make sports clothing, which would help people who exercise in very cold or very hot climates.

Clara: Really? That is amazing.

Adele: I've also read that there are other fabrics which can help reduce muscle aches and prevent us from getting ill.

Clara: Wow, that is so cool. You know, I saw a fashion show once where the designers used lights in the clothes. It was a dress made from lights. They change colour as you move.

Adele: But what was the point of that?

Clara: Well, I do agree that it's not very **practical**. I don't think many people are up for wearing a dress made of lights. It sounds like someone designed it just for the fun of it.

Adele: I'm not a fan of that idea, to be honest. It's pretty over the top! As far as I'm concerned, a dress made from lights is **useless**. Anyway, it looks like we've finally come up with some good ideas.

Clara: Yeah, I agree. So, we have clothes which are environmentally friendly, clothes which help with our health and clothes which use technology. Which one should we **focus on**?

Adele: I like the idea of clothes which help people with health problems.

Clara: Are you sure? It seems pretty complicated.

Adele: Yeah, I think it'll be fine. I do think it'll be interesting and there are a lot of different articles on the topic.

Clara: OK, let's do it!

🔊 7.2

1 a I've been reading about fashion of the future.

   b I have been reading about fashion of the future.

2 a That's amazing.

   b That is amazing.

3 a I agree that it's not very practical.

   b I do agree that it's not very practical.

4 a I think it'll be interesting.

   b I do think it'll be interesting.

🔊 7.3

1 I've been looking for an interesting topic, but to be honest, I haven't come up with anything yet.

2 And eco-friendly clothing typically helps protect the environment, too.

3 Well, these fabrics keep your body temperature the same in any kind of weather.

4 Anyway, it looks like we've finally come up with some good ideas.

5 There are a lot of different articles on the topic.

🔊 7.4

Host: In today's show, we'll be interviewing the talented fashion designer Aysha Al-Husaini. Hot on the heels of her fashion week show, Aysha's new **collection** is very popular in Doha. She got the attention of the fashion world with her **unique** designs, which **combine** traditional Muslim fashion with French chic. Aysha, thank you for coming to the studio.

Aysha: Thank you for having me.

Host: First of all, can you tell me where you get your ideas from?

Aysha: Well, I come from a Muslim family. My parents are both from Qatar. I was born there, but then we travelled a lot. I went to school in New York and I went to a design school there. These days, I spend my time travelling between Qatar and the United States.

7.5

Host: How did you feel about growing up in New York?

Aysha: Well, as a teenager in New York, I had a lot of problems trying to dress in a **modest** way. For example, when you look at summer fashion in New York, the trend is always to wear skirts, shorts and sleeveless shirts. I didn't feel comfortable wearing them, but at the same time my friends thought it was strange to wear long sleeves and jeans in the summer. So I've always tried to combine my culture with fashion. As a teenager, I would make my own clothes, like colourful skirts and scarves. I wanted my designs to be **individual**. They were unique and, eventually, people **admired** my clothes rather than laughed at me.

Host: I see. So, do you know what ideas most people have about Muslim clothes?

Aysha: Well, I think there's a lot of misunderstanding about Muslim clothes. The thing is that when you say *Muslim fashion*, people in New York think of a *burka*. You know, like the blue or black cloaks which cover women from head to toe.

Host: And could you explain what you think Muslim fashion is?

Aysha: Let me give you an example. When I first started at design school, my teachers would ask me strange questions, such as how I was going to stay in the fashion business if I'm not going to design miniskirts or sleeveless shirts. But as far as I'm concerned, there is much more to fashion than showing your body. There are millions of Muslim women who live in the United States and Europe who want to wear fashionable clothes. There are also women who simply like to dress in a modest way.

Host: So, are you saying that there is a need for fashionable clothes for Muslim women?

Aysha: Absolutely. We want to be fashionable and be ourselves at the same time. My feeling is this: I want to create clothes which are modest, but at the same time, give women **confidence** – clothes which allow women to be themselves.

Host: I see what you mean. So, how would you describe your **style**?

Aysha: Well, many reviewers have described my style as 'traditional chic', and I guess I'd agree with them. What I think is that combining traditional with chic is a huge area in fashion. I keep my eye on the fashion trends in other countries. When you look at the works of other designers in China and India, you can see that many traditional styles are being reused by young designers. Above all, people like to be individuals and show their cultural roots – they like to show where they come from.

Host: As I understand it, your designs are must-haves for Muslim women outside the United States as well. Could you tell me more about that?

Aysha: Yes. In addition to New York and Paris, I sell my collection in big cities like Doha, Dubai and Abu Dhabi. Another thing is that I also receive requests for my clothes from women in Pakistan, Indonesia, Singapore and Malaysia, so someday I might open stores there.

Host: Well, I hope you decide to go for it! That would make a lot of women around the world very happy. So, Aysha, thank you for coming to the studio today.

Aysha: It was my pleasure. Anytime!

7.6

Host: In today's show, we'll be interviewing the talented fashion designer Aysha Al-Husaini. Hot on the heels of her fashion week show, Aysha's new **collection** is very popular in Doha. She got the attention of the fashion world with her **unique** designs, which **combine** traditional Muslim fashion with French chic. Aysha, thank you for coming to the studio.

Aysha: Thank you for having me.

Host: First of all, can you tell me where you get your ideas from?

Aysha: Well, I come from a Muslim family. My parents are both from Qatar. I was born there, but then we travelled a lot. I went to school in New York and I went to a design school there. These days, I spend my time travelling between Qatar and the United States.

Host: How did you feel about growing up in New York?

Aysha: Well, as a teenager in New York, I had a lot of problems trying to dress in a **modest** way. For example, when you look at summer fashion in New York, the trend is always to wear skirts, shorts and sleeveless shirts. I didn't feel comfortable wearing them, but at the same time my friends thought it was strange to wear long sleeves and jeans in the summer. So I've always tried to combine my culture with fashion. As a teenager, I would make my own clothes, like colourful skirts and scarves. I wanted my designs to be **individual**. They were unique and eventually people **admired** my clothes rather than laughed at me.

Host: I see. So, do you know what ideas most people have about Muslim clothes?

Aysha: Well, I think there's a lot of misunderstanding about Muslim clothes. The thing is that when you say *Muslim fashion*, people in New York think of a *burka*. You know, like the blue or black cloaks which cover women from head to toe.

Host: And could you explain what you think Muslim fashion is?

Aysha: Let me give you an example. When I first started at design school, my teachers would ask me strange questions, such as how I was going to stay in the fashion business if I'm not going to design miniskirts or sleeveless shirts. But as far as I'm concerned, there is much more to fashion than showing your body. There are millions of Muslim women who live in the United States and Europe who want to wear fashionable clothes. There are also women who simply like to dress in a modest way.

Host: So, are you saying that there is a need for fashionable clothes for Muslim women?

Aysha: Absolutely. We want to be fashionable and be ourselves at the same time. My feeling is this: I want to create clothes which are modest, but at the same time, give women **confidence** – clothes which allow women to be themselves.

Host: I see what you mean. So, how would you describe your **style**?

Aysha: Well, many reviewers have described my style as 'traditional chic', and I guess I'd agree with them. What I think is that combining traditional with chic is a huge area in fashion. I keep my eye on the fashion trends in other countries. When you look at the works of other designers in China and India, you can see that many traditional styles are being reused by young designers. Above all, people like to be individuals and show their cultural roots – they like to show where they come from.

Host: As I understand it, your designs are must-haves for Muslim women outside the United States as well. Could you tell me more about that?

Aysha: Yes. In addition to New York and Paris, I sell my collection in big cities like Doha, Dubai and Abu Dhabi. Another thing is that I also receive requests for my clothes from women in Pakistan, Indonesia, Singapore and Malaysia, so someday I might open stores there.

Host: Well, I hope you decide to go for it! That would make a lot of women around the world very happy. So, Aysha, thank you for coming to the studio today.

Aysha: It was my pleasure. Anytime!

UNIT 8
▶ Workshops for entrepreneurs

Reporter: When Marie LaQuerre got laid off, she had an idea to make and sell a line of children's novelties.

Marie LaQuerre: My company name is actually Goobity Goo.

Reporter: What she didn't have was thousands of dollars to buy a laser cutter to create her products.

Marie LaQuerre: That machine can do, like, everything, it seems like.

Reporter: The day the iPad was announced, Patrick Buckley had an idea for a custom-made cover. What he didn't have was the expensive, computerized woodcutting machine he needed to produce a prototype. LaQuerre, Buckley and scores of other budding entrepreneurs have become members of TechShop in Menlo Park, California, a place for do-it-yourselfers, inventors and dreamers.

Mark Hatch: We believe that every kitchen should come with compressed air, electricity and a vice.

Reporter: Mark Hatch is TechShop's CEO.

Mark Hatch: Most don't. You know, people get to come here and use ours.

Reporter: Here's the drill. Joining TechShop is a little like joining a health club, except here, for $100 a month, instead of running on a treadmill, you get to run industrial-strength machinery. Members have access to the latest in computer-assisted design and machine tools that would cost a fortune to buy.

Mark Hatch: We teach people in an afternoon how to make things. We have a lot of entrepreneurs.

Reporter: With the tools at TechShop, Phil Hughes developed a way to cool computer servers that could save vast amounts of energy.

Phil Hughes: This pulls at it. All the heat is at the server, from the server to the lid.

Reporter: For now, his company, Clustered Systems, has its world headquarters at TechShop. But a partnership with Emerson, the huge appliance manufacturer, could change that.

Phil Hughes: They expect to sell thousands and thousands of these things, which is going to make us very happy.

Reporter: And perhaps very rich?

Phil Hughes: Well, yes. Why not?

Reporter: For $100 a month another member is building a lunar landing module for an XPrize competition.

Man: Where else can I find someplace I can store my lunar lander?

Reporter: Marie LaQuerre is now selling her products online and in a few retail stores. Patrick Buckley's iPad cover is taking off and 30 people have been hired to make it.

Patrick Buckley: We're on track to do between $3 and $5 million this year.

Reporter: And TechShop is doing well too, expanding to eight more locations. Evidence that in America today, money may be tight, but ideas and ambition are flowing freely.

🔊 8.1

In this week's programme, I'd like to talk about a book that has changed the way I think about money. It's called *The Secret of Being Wealthy*. It was written by a business school graduate named John Holm who decided to study the behaviour of wealthy people. He paid close attention to what rich people do: checking where they eat, what they buy, how they live and so on. The results of his study were pretty surprising.

🔊 8.2

When you think of someone who is very rich, what comes to mind? Most people think that rich people live lavish lifestyles – that is, they drive very expensive cars, eat in expensive restaurants, own a yacht or live in big houses. But, as John Holm discovered, people who have money don't actually do these things. Most **millionaires** actually seem to have ordinary lifestyles. In other words, they have normal cars, average houses and so on. On the other hand, people who *look* rich – the people who drive the latest Ferrari or only wear designer clothes – may not actually be rich at all. Instead, they have spent all their money trying to show off – showing other people that they might be wealthy. In other words, having expensive things is not always a sign that someone is rich.

So, what do millionaires do and what can we learn from them? Well, millionaires are often financially savvy. To put it another way, they're smart about how to save and spend money. The first important thing is that millionaires always have a good handle on their budget. In other words, they know how much they're spending. According to Holm, around 75 percent of millionaires know exactly how much money they have and they know exactly how much they spend on food, bills, clothes, etc. As a result, they don't spend too much and they don't get into **debt**. They can plan for the future and save their money. To sum up, the lesson here is that you should never spend more money than you have!

Another surprising fact is that millionaires usually have simple lifestyles. They have nice houses and nice cars, but they don't spend all their money on these things. In fact, most rich people stay in the same place for a very long time and don't live in big, expensive palaces. Indeed, according to John Holm, half of millionaires have lived in the same house for 20 years. Also, around 65 percent of millionaires live in homes which cost around the national average. Again, the important lesson here is to live within your means – that is, don't spend more money than you have. If you spend all your **savings** on a luxury BMW, then you probably aren't rich – you just want to look rich. In fact, the study reveals that 86 percent of luxury cars are bought by people who can't **afford** them. Most rich people don't have bank **loans** – they only spend a small percentage of what they have and they save or invest the rest.

Now here is an interesting fact. The study shows that most millionaires have very happy relationships. Not only are they married, but they stay married for a long time. In John Holm's opinion, this is very important because of the golden rule about **saving money**. There is no doubt that it's more difficult to save money if you are single. One effect of being a couple is that it's easier to save money. If there are two of you, it's easier to pay attention to what money you have and what you're spending.

And of course, people who don't have huge bank loans and debts are happier. If you don't have to worry about the monthly credit card **payments**, you're less likely to buy things to make you feel better. People with debt often spend more time shopping, just to make themselves feel happier, but real millionaires don't need to do this.

So, what can we learn from the wealthy? The answer is surprisingly simple. Don't spend more money than you have. Don't get into debt or take out bank loans. Pay close attention to your money and don't spend time trying to show other people that you're rich. In John Holm's opinion, being 'wealthy' is a feeling. That is, it doesn't mean being rich or having millions. It means being happy with what you have.

🔊 8.3

1 Most people think that rich people live lavish lifestyles, that is they drive very expensive cars, eat in expensive restaurants, own a yacht or live in big houses.

2 In other words, having expensive things is not always a sign that someone is rich.

3 On the other hand, people who look rich – the people who drive the latest Ferrari or only wear designer clothes – may not actually be rich at all.

4 As a result, they don't spend too much and they don't get into debt.

5 There is no doubt that it's more difficult to save money if you are single.

6 So, what can we learn from the wealthy? The answer is surprisingly simple.

🔊 8.4

Host: In today's programme, we discuss the recent **decision** made by several universities to give students money in return for good grades. Students will be paid by the hour to take additional Maths and Science classes. The students who improve their grades and keep their grade average high will be given cash rewards at the end of each term. To discuss this new project, we have invited education expert Dr Michael Burns and we welcome your calls during the programme. We'd like to hear your opinion: Do you think university students should be paid for good grades?

🔊 8.5

Host: Dr Burns, thank you for coming today. Can you tell us more about the project? Where does this idea come from?

Dr Burns: Thank you. Well, the idea of paying students for their work isn't new. For example, students in Denmark are paid about €760 a month to attend university. They receive the payments for a maximum of six years, starting at the age of 18.

The goal of paying students is to **encourage** them to finish their education and be able to get a good job in the future.

Host: I see. Let's hear from our first caller. Mariam Hassan is the president of a medium-sized university. Dr Hassan?

Dr Hassan: Hello. Yes, I recently read about this new programme and I really don't think it's a good idea. I understand that many students drop out of university because of financial problems. At my university alone, the dropout rate is over 25 percent. However, will paying students really encourage them to continue? In my experience, it won't. Of course, the statistics are terrible, but I'm not confident that this programme will solve the real problems – it may just cover them up. I think the money would be better spent on student **services**, like hiring additional professors and advisors. Two of the reasons why students drop out are stress and poor time management. Advisors can help students learn to **manage** their time better. As a consequence, students will do better at university and will be more likely to graduate.

Dr Burns: I can see your point, but we have already spent a lot on student services. I think that paying students to study will show them that we treat them like adults. It will give them a **sense** of responsibility. University students are young adults and so, when they have a choice between staying at university and studying or going to work and making money, they often make the wrong choice. They want to have money so that they can buy things for themselves. Besides, we don't want to pay them a lot. I think we're simply giving them an option: stay at university and be paid or get a **minimum wage** job.

Host: Christine Thorne is a parent with two children at university.

Mrs Thorne: Hello. I was very worried when I heard about this new programme. I realize that students need encouragement to stay at university, but are we going in the right direction? First of all, I feel that we're sending the students the wrong message. Learning should be about studying new things and being **responsible**. Personally, I think the students who aren't interested in studying will simply take the easy courses to keep their average grade high and get the cash. I believe that we should focus more on rewarding excellent universities and teachers and not on students who might be lazy.

Dr Burns: These are all good points, but I don't think that this view applies to all students. Not all parents are educated or interested in studying. They pass this bad attitude on to their own children. Then the children don't see the benefits of learning. To change this image, we need to show them a good reason for studying.

Host: Thank you. Let's have a look now at some of the comments we've received during the programme.

🔊 8.6

Host: Dr Burns, thank you for coming today. Can you tell us more about the project? Where does this idea come from?

Dr Burns: Thank you. Well, the idea of paying students for their work isn't new. For example, students in Denmark are paid about €760 a month to attend university. They receive the payments for a maximum of six years, starting at the age of 18. The goal of paying students is to encourage them to finish their education and be able to get a good job in the future.

Host: I see. Let's hear from our first caller. Mariam Hassan is the president of a medium-sized university. Dr Hassan?

Dr Hassan: Hello. Yes, I recently read about this new programme and I really don't think it's a good idea. I understand that many students drop out of university because of financial problems. At my university alone, the dropout rate is over 25 percent. However, will paying students really encourage them to continue? In my experience, it won't. Of course, the statistics are terrible, but I'm not confident that this programme will solve the real problems – it may just cover them up. I think the money would be better spent on student services, like hiring additional professors and advisors. Two of the reasons why students drop out are stress and poor time management. Advisors can help students learn to manage their time better. As a consequence, students will do better at university and will be more likely to graduate.

ACKNOWLEDGEMENTS

The authors and publishers acknowledge the following sources of copyright material and are grateful for the permissions granted. While every effort has been made, it has not always been possible to identify the sources of all the material used, or to trace all copyright holders. If any omissions are brought to our notice, we will be happy to include the appropriate acknowledgements on reprinting and in the next update to the digital edition, as applicable.

Key: T = Top, B = Below, L = Left, R = Right, TR = Top Right, BL = Below Left, BR = Below Right, TL = Top Left.

Photos

All below images are sourced from Getty Images.

pp. 14–15: Katiekk2/iStock/Getty Images Plus; p. 20: Peter Charlesworth/LightRocket; p. 21: jpbcpa/E+; p. 26 (L): Daniel J Cox/Oxford Scientific; p. 26 (C): Olaf Kruger; p. 26 (R): Andy Rouse/The Image Bank; pp. 36–37:Bloomberg; p. 41: YOSHIKAZU TSUNO/AFP; p. 42 (a): Richard Allenby-Pratt/arabianEye; p. 42 (b): tanukiphoto/E+; p. 42 (c): Jeff Greenberg/Universal Images Group; p. 42 (d): FroukjeBrouwer/iStock/Getty Images Plus; p. 42 (e): Kenishirotie/iStock/Getty Images Plus; p. 42 (f): Hero Images; p. 43: The Asahi Shimbun; p. 47: ARIS MESSINIS/AFP; pp. 58–59: DKart/E+; p. 63: Jeff Greenberg/Photolibrary; p. 66 (L): specnaz-s/iStock/Getty Images Plus; p. 66 (R): Peter Dazeley/Photographer's Choice; p. 70: Ollie Millington/Getty Images News; p. 71: Frédéric Soltan/Corbis News; p. 73: Roberto Westbrook/Blend Images; p. 77: Jordan Siemens/Iconica; pp. 80–81: Suttipong Sutiratanachai/Moment; p. 86: Hero Images; p. 93: Eric Audras/ONOKY; p. 106 (L): Igor-Kardasov/iStock/Getty Images Plus; p. 106 (R): Image Source; p. 107 (L): Image Source RF/Raphye Alexius; p. 107 (R): Image Source; p. 110: bpablo/E+; p. 113 (L): Carlos Osorio/Toronto Star; p. 113 (R): Hero Images; p. 115 (taekwondo): Drazen/E+; p. 115 (team sports):Thomas Barwick/Taxi; p. 115 (cycling): monkeybusinessimages/iStock/Getty Images Plus; p. 115 (acupuncture): Bridget Borsheim/Stockbyte; pp. 124–125: Steven Vidler/Travelpix; p. 129 (a): Dave King; p. 129 (c): DEA/A. DAGLI ORTI/De Agostini; p. 132 (R): View Stock; p. 136: ahmetemre/iStock/Getty Images Plus; p. 140 (TL): pagadesign/E+; p. 140 (TR): scanrail/iStock/Getty Images Plus; p. 140 (BL): 3alexd/E+; p. 140 (BR): Rawpixel/iStock/Getty Images Plus; pp. 146–147: Samir Hussein/WireImages; p. 150 (L): TOSHIFUMI KITAMURA/AFP; p. 150 (R): Chung Sung-Jun/Getty Images News; p. 157: Pete Saloutos/Image Source; p. 164: MANAN VATSYAYANA/AFP; p. 165: DGLimages/iStock/Getty Images Plus; pp. 168–169: Digital Vision/Photodisc; p. 173: DeltaOFF/iStock/Getty Images Plus; pp. 174–175: Paul Williams – Funkystock/imageBROKER; p. 176: lovelyday12/iStock/Getty Images Plus; p. 180: Reza Estakhrian/Stone; p. 187: DreamPictures/Shannon Faulk/Blend Images.

The following images are sourced from other libraries:
p. 48: Peteri/Shutterstock; pp. 102–103: frans lemmens/Alamy Stock Photos; p. 129 (b): Sergey Goruppa/Shutterstock; p. 129 (d): Nataliya Hora/Shutterstock; p. 132 (L): Triff/Shutterstock; p. 132 (C): Lotus_studio/Shutterstock; p. 142: Vitaly Korovin/Shutterstock.

Front cover photography by sprokop/iStock/Getty Images Plus.

Video stills

All below stills are sourced from Getty Images.

p. 82 (video 1, video 2, video 3): AFP; p. 82 (video 4): topnatthapon/Creatas Video; p. 104: ITN; p. 148: Crane.tv – Footage/Getty Images Editorial Footage.

The following stills are sourced from other libraries:
p. 16, p. 38, p. 60, p. 126, p. 170: BBC Worldwide Learning.

Illustrations

p. 24: Clive Goodyer; p. 41: Fiona Gowen; p. 85: Ben Hasler (NB Illustrations).

Videos

All below clips are sourced from Getty Images and BBC Worldwide Learning

AFP Footage; topnatthapon/Creatas Video; kickimages/Creatas Video+/Getty Images Plus; Faithfulshot; ITN; Sky News/Film Image Partner; Tribune Broadcasting – Fabiola Franco; ITN; Wazee Archiva/Archive Films: Editorial; Roger Maynard – Footage; Press association; Bloomberg Video – Footage/Bloomberg; Feature Story News – Footage/Getty Images Editorial Footage; Crane.tv – Footage/Getty Images Editorial Footage; BBC Motion Gallery Editorial/BBC News; Skyworks Places/Image Bank Film; Gorlov/Creatas Video+/Getty Images Plus; Multi-bits/Image bank film; BBC Worldwide Learning.

Corpus

Development of this publication has made use of the Cambridge English Corpus (CEC). The CEC is a multi-billion word computer database of contemporary spoken and written English. It includes British English, American English and other varieties of English. It also includes the Cambridge Learner Corpus, developed in collaboration with the University of Cambridge ESOL Examinations. Cambridge University Press has built up the CEC to provide evidence about language use that helps to produce better language teaching materials.

Cambridge Dictionaries

Cambridge dictionaries are the world's most widely used dictionaries for learners of English. The dictionaries are available in print and online at dictionary.cambridge.org. Copyright © Cambridge University Press, reproduced with permission.

Typeset by emc design ltd.

UNLOCK SECOND EDITION ADVISORY PANEL

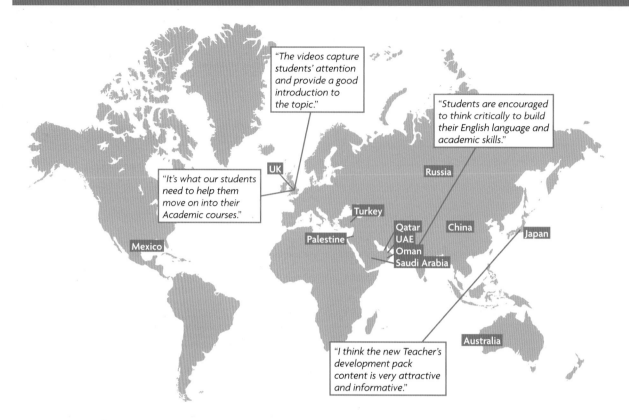

"The videos capture students' attention and provide a good introduction to the topic."

"Students are encouraged to think critically to build their English language and academic skills."

"It's what our students need to help them move on into their Academic courses."

"I think the new Teacher's development pack content is very attractive and informative."

UK · Russia · Turkey · Qatar · UAE · Oman · Saudi Arabia · China · Japan · Mexico · Palestine · Australia

We would like to thank the following ELT professionals all around the world for their support, expertise and input throughout the development of *Unlock* Second Edition:

Adnan Abu Ayyash, Birzeit University, Palestine	Takayuki Hara, Kagoshima University, Japan	Megan Putney, Dhofar University, Oman
Bradley Adrain, University of Queensland, Australia	Esengül Hasdemir, Atilim University, Turkey	Wayne Rimmer, United Kingdom
Sarah Ali, Nottingham Trent International College (NTIC), United Kingdom	Irina Idilova, Moscow Institute of Physics and Technology, Russia	Sana Salam, TED University, Turkey
Ana Maria Astiazaran, Colegio Regis La Salle, Mexico	Meena Inguva, Sultan Qaboos University, Oman	Setenay Şekercioglu, Işık University, Turkey
Asmaa Awad, University of Sharjah, United Arab Emirates	Vasilios Konstantinidis, Prince Sultan University, Kingdom of Saudi Arabia	Robert B. Staehlin, Morioka University, Japan
Jesse Balanyk, Zayed University, United Arab Emirates	Andrew Leichsenring, Tamagawa University, Japan	Yizhi Tang, Xueersi English, TAL Group, China
Lenise Butler, Universidad del Valle de México, Mexico	Alexsandra Minic, Modern College of Business and Science, Oman	Valeria Thomson, Muscat College, Oman
Esin Çağlayan, Izmir University of Economics, Turkey	Daniel Newbury, Fuji University, Japan	Amira Traish, University of Sharjah, United Arab Emirates
Matthew Carey, Qatar University, Qatar	Güliz Özgürel, Yaşar University, Turkey	Poh Leng Wendelkin, INTO London, United Kingdom
Eileen Dickens, Universidad de las Américas, Mexico	Özlem Perks, Istanbul Ticaret University, Turkey	Yoee Yang, The Affiliated High School of SCNU, China
Mireille Bassam Farah, United Arab Emirates	Claudia Piccoli, Harmon Hall, Mexico	Rola Youhia, University of Adelaide College, Australia
Adriana Ghoul, Arab American University, Palestine	Tom Pritchard, University of Edinburgh, United Kingdom	Long Zhao, Xueersi English, TAL Group, China
Burçin Gönülsen, Işık University, Turkey		